PARK LEARNING CENTRE

The Park Cheltenham
Gloucestershire GL50 2RH
Telephone: 01242 714333

UNIVERSITY OF
GLOUCESTERSHIRE
at Cheltenham and Gloucester

NORMAL LOAN

Managing Without Power

Also by this author

Management Teams: why they succeed or fail
Team Roles at Work
The Coming Shape of Organization
Changing the Way We Work
Beyond the Team
How to Build Successful Teams... The Belbin Way (CD-ROM)

The author may be contacted at:

Belbin Associates
3–4 Bennell Court
West Street
Comberton
Cambridge
CB3 7DS, UK
Tel: +44-(0)1223-264975
Fax: +44-(0)1223-264976
www.belbin.com
info@belbin.com

Managing Without Power

Gender relationships in the story of human evolution

R. Meredith Belbin

BUTTERWORTH
HEINEMANN

OXFORD AUCKLAND BOSTON JOHANNESBURG MELBOURNE NEW DELHI

Butterworth-Heinemann
Linacre House, Jordan Hill, Oxford OX2 8DP
225 Wildwood Avenue, Woburn, MA 01801-2041
A division of Reed Educational and Professional Publishing Ltd

℞ A member of the Reed Elsevier plc group

First published 2001

British Library Cataloguing in Publication Data
Belbin, R. M.
    Managing without power: gender relationships in the story
    of human evolution
    1. Social evolution – Sex differences   2. Power (Social
    sciences) – Sex differences   3. Sexual division of labour –
    Psychological aspects   4. Sex role – History
    I. Title
    304.5

ISBN 0 7506 5192 X

Composition by Genesis Typesetting, Rochester, Kent
Printed and bound in Great Britain by Biddles Ltd
www.biddles.co.uk

FOR EVERY TITLE THAT WE PUBLISH, BUTTERWORTH-HEINEMANN
WILL PAY FOR BTCV TO PLANT AND CARE FOR A TREE.

Contents

Contents

Preface

This book diverges from the theme for which I am perhaps better known, being the written form of some presentations I have given to various management groups. In the past my focus has fallen on the importance of team roles for establishing how people can best work together in order to achieve a common objective. The strategy and methods associated with team roles have travelled widely and taken root in many cultures. One related question I have often been asked is how well the concept of team roles applies across the gender gap. Were women more disposed towards some team roles than others? Did men and women fall into different patterns? I tried to reply as best as I could. I would point out that women, like men, have distinguished themselves in every one of the nine team roles and that if different gender patterns did arise there could be other reasons that were possibly responsible, like the different jobs on which men and women were engaged.

Somehow I sensed that women were not fully satisfied by the answers I gave. Some felt themselves very different from men in some indefinable way and I had not helped them to understand why. In behaviour they could learn to do what was needed, which is always important where teamwork is involved. And yet they knew that in many respects a gender gap existed in behaviour that called for deeper understanding. Was it all due to unfair discrimination or was there more to it?

It so happened at the time that I was engaged in research into the nature of work. The venture had led me to study the intricate ways in which the division of labour was organized in other species, and especially in the world of the social insects (about which I wrote in *The Coming Shape of Organization*). I could not help concluding, once my studies were completed, that human work was much less well organized and had grown from quite rudimentary beginnings. The fact of the matter is that the earliest division of labour in the human species was gender-based. Men and women did different work and have continued to do so ever since. How then had that gender-related division of labour become transformed into a pattern of employment that is supposedly becoming gender-free? And so I set myself the challenge of trying to answer that question. The result is this book, which sets out to examine the roles of women in relation to the roles adopted by men at different stages of human evolution.

Differing physical endowments have rendered women the 'weaker sex', which means that gender-relationships are always liable to imbalance. It follows that if women are to progress to whatever gives them personal fulfilment and if they are to make their due contribution to the wider society, the first need is to tackle the problem of Power. How far Power is centralized or shared, used or abused ultimately acts as a barometer of how women fare in society as a whole. And it is not only they who have a special interest in curtailing Power. We are now moving into an era where the destructive effects of Power far exceed those advantages that it conferred at an earlier period. We are obliged to confess that humans are one of those rare species that kill in large numbers members of their own kind.

> Nature is red in tooth and claw
> Humans are red in sword and war

The exercise of Power has manifested itself throughout recorded history in bloodshed. But its ill effects are not solely confined to blood-letting. Power has exercised its grip in many other ways. Over-centralized control alienates people and results in many diseconomies in social organization. The barrenness of that approach is encountering increased resistance. The Big Leader no longer commands unquestioning support. Yet while human society is evolving in a new direction at a gathering pace, it is also caught between two eras. It has not fully escaped from the past nor has it ventured very far through the portals of the era that is beckoning. So in order that we may understand this transitional phase I have attempted to put into perspective the evolutionary process, starting at the beginning and taking us to the present and beyond.

It is my belief that humans have never ceased to evolve and have been as subject to the laws of Evolution as any other creature. The path has twisted and turned in patterns that have seldom been recognized. In the earliest period of human society physical forms facilitated certain types of function. So successful was this adaptation that human populations grew to outstrip their ideal habitat. They migrated to new lands, adapted to local conditions and spread throughout the world. But in due course population growth could not be solved by dispersal. Expansion became blocked as populations found and then settled on the best territories. The would-be expansionists could only secure favoured territories by carrying out offensives against existing occupiers. So survival of the fittest now rewarded successful aggression. The formula which made this possible comprised two factors – aggression in the human psyche combined with the propensity to operate in large numbers under the control of a directive commander. Civilization has been largely built up on this tested formula. That is because large groups outfight small groups and can draw on a wider range of resources to tackle big projects. Yet in their eventual victory large groups lose out in other ways. Through personal experience in the study of teams I was to discover that teams behaved very differently from groups. The former emerged as the more effective in deploying human talent. What primarily differentiated teams from groups was size. The intimacy of the team, one learns, is soon lost as it expands into a group. And as it does so, the propensity for engaging in rotating leadership is lost and its democratic ethos disappears. One person rises to take charge and becomes the major player. And as groups expand in size, a further change in their character takes place. Leaders become rulers and eventually tyrants. To consolidate their position they establish their hold through the self-perpetuating procedures of *command and control*. Ultimately I sensed a connection between these observed processes and the unfolding of historical events that have so often resulted in setbacks and even catastrophes for humanity.

This book examines the past and its genetic legacy on human behaviour in the present era. The theme is that the world has passed through two distinct phases and is about to enter a third. In the first era a balance existed within small communities. Men were bonded together in hunting parties and men and women were bonded in their interpersonal relationships. It was an intricate social network that could yield consensus. That balance was destroyed as population pressures ultimately produced a mismatch between people and resources. Evolution was now to take a new direction as the struggle for territory became paramount. The outcome depended on the male capacity to exercise and compete for Power against other groups. During this second era, covering almost all recorded history, the status and social contribution of women in society became inversely related to the pursuit of Power. Ruthless Power ultimately led to the degradation of women as well as to vast loss of life. That era is coming to an end for reasons that will be described. And as the exercise of Power declines, the social prominence of women will reappear to mirror its former importance. In this third era the advancement of women and the relative weakening in the position of men will complicate the social and political agenda of our times.

How will men react to some loss in their traditional role? Will women break through the 'glass ceiling' and, if so, will they learn to manage in a distinctly feminine way? Will they regain the status and influence they enjoyed in primaeval society? In this world of changing gender relationships what are the principal shifts in management style that can be foreseen and are to be recommended? What are the lessons that both women and men can learn from the story of human evolution?

Before I begin the narrative I would like to say that I have had to start from somewhere and would declare how much I owe to those who have charted the intellectual way ahead. I owe a debt to several authors: the Oxford geneticist, the late C.D. Darlington whose comprehensive study of world history demonstrated that culture has a genetic base; Desmond Morris, the zoologist who examined humans from an entirely new perspective; Robert Ardrey, who revealed the struggle for territory as a prime force in the evolution of all species; David Quamman, for extending Darwinian theory through his studies of extinction; Jarred Diamond, for the breadth of his understanding of the evolutionary process; and finally E.O. Wilson, for his approach in finding significant new configurations in the biological world. These and others I have listed as recommended reading at the end of this book. There is, however, a wealth of historical reading matter that might well have been included in this list which I have decided to omit. That is not to deny how much I owe to an intensive study of world history. But because my focus has been on common patterns I concluded that detailed historical references would distract the reader from the hoped-for clarity in theme this book is intended to deliver.

Lastly, I want to record how grateful I am to my colleagues Liz Godfrey, Peter Lancaster and Tom Robson who have selflessly afforded me their help and advice; and to my wife, Eunice, for much appreciated correction and guidance in steering me in the direction intended. And finally I was very glad to enrol the services of the cartoonist Steve Chadburn, who has helped make fun of the whole thing. Cartoons combine light relief and truth. Without his illustrations this book would have been a grimmer story.

M.B.
January 2001

Introduction

We learn from Palaeoanthropology that the earliest known humans lived about 180,000 years ago. Their anatomy was indistinguishable from their descendants today. Just suppose such an ancestor with an appropriate hair styling and a suitable set of clothes were to walk down the street, would anyone regard the stranger as odd? The evidence suggests that there would be nothing remarkable on which an observer might comment. But when it comes to behaviour, more thought-provoking issues arise. Suppose one had the services of a time machine capable of swapping babies between millennia, would primaeval babies grow up and ultimately behave in the same way as their modern counterparts? Conversely, would modern man and woman behave like primaeval men and women if transferred at birth and brought up in primaeval society? It is a matter for speculation and most attempts at an answer either imply a belief in Adam and Eve (being the casts from which all humans are taken) or take an environmentalist view on human behaviour. In either instance, the answer to the question posed would be much the same. The line would be that human beings have not changed much, if at all. The only significant change has been one of circumstance.

Had human evolution stood still, that would be a fair response. But the alternative view developed in this book, on the basis of an intensive sifting of evidence, is that human nature has not stood still but has been modified under the relentless pressure of natural selection. Such a standpoint does no more than reaffirm the general bio-scientific principle that evolution is a continuing process. How much modification has really taken place in what has been a relatively short period of evolutionary time? Until a mere 12,000 years ago all humans lived in hunter–gatherer societies. Pre-history covers an extensive time-span, but recorded history itself covers no more than two per cent of the human story. Yet in this relatively short period the most rapid change took place in the culture of the species. So was it accompanied by an equivalent change in biologically based behavioural characteristics? The critical time-slot may not sound very significant genetically. Yet it would be wrong to infer that the rate of change is a simple function of the passage of time. We know from the evolution of other species that long periods of equilibrium can be punctuated by abrupt changes as new forms of competitive advantage came into being.

As a rule, evolution speeds up when the forces of natural selection become subject to a more than usual degree of stress. Throughout the animal kingdom extremes of drought, flooding and temperature variation all take their toll of those less fitted to survive. In the case of humans there is a unique form of stress, called war. War is actuated when one group of people sets out to exercise power over another. The losers then become subject to extinction, the victors prevail and multiply and the evolutionary process is speeded up. That chain of events needed a trigger within the community. It could only begin with the emergence of specialized power-seekers, capable of channelling the energies of their communities into territorial expansion at the expense of other peoples. This book sets out to review the nature of that process, examining its origins and probing into why it happened when it did. At the same time it will seek to examine how far the rise and fall of power has corresponded with the fluctuating status, scope and general position of women in society. Evidence from the remoter past suggests that women have succeeded in managing without power. They had to, for they could never stand up to men in muscle strength or in matching their fondness for the use of weapons. Yet they were often remarkably successful in controlling men until their position was lost as power began to play an increasingly important part in human affairs. Managing without power, as the title of this book implies, will ultimately form the focus of my attention.

Yet before I can address the challenge of this assignment, I feel it incumbent on me to remove all ambiguities that the term conveys, for the word power in everyday speech has many meanings. There is hydroelectric power along with other forms of like energy that fuel our economies. And there are those two contrasting forms of abstract cogency – unbridled power and the power of love. And in response to the claim that knowledge is power, one can see that a single word is capable of transmitting many different thoughts and associations. It is an unfortunate feature of human language that however vast the extent of human vocabulary, there is a common tendency to convert familiar words to different uses and sometimes contrasting meanings. A strong emotional distinction exists between *power over* and *power to*. Most people fight against those who try to exert *power over* them. Yet such a noun with negative connotations becomes positive as soon as it is attached to a different suffix. The *power to do* many things represents for many people a supreme aspiration.

This book gives special attention to the former sort of power. Because power, in terms of its evolutionary effects, is pivotal to the theme of this book I have underscored its special meaning by signifying power over with the capital letter P. So the Age of Power relates to that era of history when Power can be deemed the operating force in exerting its particular effects on human evolution. Power becomes a factor with a special potency whenever one human being holds sway over another by dint of force or its threat. Throughout much of recorded human history, masters have owned slaves, wielding Power that was absolute. Slaves could be killed or maltreated because the slave lacked any means of protection or means of appeal. Slaves were kept only because they were useful. The memory of slavery lingers on because it evokes a cause over which reformers fought for many years. But there were other victims of Power, defeated in battle or put down after rebellion, who were deemed not to be useful and so were killed in vast numbers rather than enslaved. They and their descendants did not survive, whereas the descendants of the victors did. We must remember the identity of both groups who took part in a drama that unfolded over thousands of years. Biologically, its dramatic effects have stamped their psychogenetic mark on the human character through a process called natural selection.

Prior to the Age of Power, natural selection had followed another path governed by the development of physical characteristics finely attuned to promote survival in a given environment. The threads of these two Ages, centred on physical and psychogenetic evolution, have been put together to present a concise narrative. The story takes us on to the third Age upon which humanity has now entered. For the purposes of approaching this difficult and challenging assignment I have conducted an extensive study of world history and consulted a great deal of biological, zoological, anthropological and archaeological material. Yet I will spare the reader from retracing these steps or documenting them. The reason is that the intended theme of this book deals with the processes rather than facts in their isolation and inevitably rests on a personal interpretation of the material. Others might take a different view. Should they do so, that is fine, for the road to intellectual progress is never clear-cut or undisputed.

Before I begin in earnest, a few words need to be said about the assumptions and methods underlying my approach. This book is written with the perspective of an evolutionist and in this respect I have taken an essentially orthodox line. In order to clarify this, a few interlocking principles need to be explained at the outset.

The first principle is that of biological utility. In Evolution physical changes, differentiating one species from another, have a functional significance within the environmental niche occupied by that species. Changes do not endure unless they serve some useful purpose. Allied to the concept of biological utility is the relationship between form and function, which work closely together. If function is lost, form and its capacity tend to be lost also. Birds on islands devoid of predators lose their capacity for flight; fish in caves their capacity for sight. So it is with humans. The physical features of humans are full of meaning, even if by contemporary standards those features have only a vestigial significance. Even so, that significance can be reconstructed. Another linked concept to guide one's interpretation is the conservation of energy. Nature does not waste energy on activities that have no biological benefits; and if it appears to do so, the likely reason is that the biological advantage has not been grasped.

The second principle that underlines the themes of this book is that biological utility relates to behavioural as much as to physical characteristics. Temperament, interests and aptitudes have no discernible physical correlates. There are no physical features that enable observers to differentiate the mass murderer and rapist from the charity worker. Evolution has been working on us all with an unseen hand. The distinguishing features of DNA may be traced along historical routes but, given the present state of knowledge, the behavioural genes themselves defy detection. Yet it does not matter too much that the whole picture is not complete. One is aware of the existence of the behavioural genes and the importance of their outcomes, the more especially as a result of findings from studies of twins. In spite of separation at birth and in upbringing, identical twins have been revealed as possessing remarkable similarities in behaviour. If the tendency to behave in idiosyncratic ways is genetically implanted, one is left to wonder how one accounts for the wide variation between individuals in the general population. How have such diversities in behaviour come about? These questions prompt the inquiry into whether individual differences have an evolutionary meaning.

To reach the present day human genetic inheritance has taken a long and tortuous path. The positive outcome is that the foundation has been laid for a complex civilized society. But the downside is that this journey has also brought with it much genetic baggage that has outlived its purpose and now threatens to cancel many of the gains made. Before we can weigh up the balance and consider what remedial strategies are possible, we need to understand our own genetic story. Only then can we hope to manage what is bequeathed to us in coping with the issues of the future.

PART ONE

THE AGE OF RESPECT

Preview

Primaeval society was built around the economy of the hunter–gatherer and involved a division of labour based on the separate functional worlds of men and women. Yet that division produced a balanced community due to the complementary nature of the roles to which men and women were disposed. The specific character of human sexual activity, being much in excess of that required for procreation, served an additional evolutionary purpose, tying men and women together in a continuous relationship in the interests of the community as a whole. As contributors to that community, men could rely on their greater brawn. Women, for their part, were esteemed as the givers of life. In addition, their contribution to the economy as gatherers was as great or greater than that of men as hunters. The lesser physical strength of women was counterbalanced by an ability to manipulate men through the level of their communication and psycho-sexual skills. Women could manage without power. Religion was based on respect (and awe) for Nature.

But with the dispersal of the primaeval community from its original habitat, men increased their relative contribution to the economy by further developing their hunting and fishing skills, so extending their influence over the community. As humans fanned out over land and water, Evolution took a new turn. Natural selection produced strains of humans with differing physical characteristics and personal attributes to match the challenge of different environments. Some engaged in the Great Migration travelled great distances by water, developing a depth of understanding of Nature and of Physics, Mathematics and Astronomy in the process. Migrants generally avoided the settlements of others and the consequent possibility of conflict in competition for territory. On the other hand, once established, newly settled communities explored trade and social contacts to mutual advantage.

In the beginning

Recorded human history bears the stamp of continuing violence at such a level that any detached observer might well conclude that humans are the most dangerous of all creatures, being ever prone to engage in conflicts with their own kind. But was it always so? And if it was not, what does it tell us about the future? Can some of the behaviour of former times be rekindled? Or have men and women been cast in some supposed mould, like Adam and Eve, in which human behaviour is forever locked? Are humans destined to repeat the mistakes to which they are genetically prone, so that the concept of human social progress might be largely illusory?

Before one can address such arresting questions, the first need is to look back into the past in order to understand what has evolved and why. If recurring modes of human behaviour have genetic roots, to scrutinize them demands a journey back in time beyond the earliest historical records. Yet that is the trail to follow, however difficult it may be, if light is to be thrown on those basic issues that threaten the future of mankind. The only means of understanding the earliest humans is to reconstruct their behaviour. Hence it is incumbent on us to examine fragments of evidence, for that is all we have, and to piece these together as best we can.

The concept of biological utility, as it relates to the distinctive nature of the human form, offers a good starting-point for the inquiry. Zoologists take the view that function follows form and particular forms develop because they offer a significant advantage in the struggle for survival. That is the lesson Evolution teaches. So do those basic laws of Nature apply equally to *Homo sapiens?* And if they do, is there a convincing explanation of the human form?

The first need therefore is to scrutinize human physical characteristics in relation to function. At first sight the approach does not look very promising. *Homo sapiens* himself does not cut a very convincing figure. In many ways he looks less fitted to survive than his one-time contemporaneous hominid, known as *Neanderthal man*. The latter was more robustly built, stronger and heavier, and evidently adept at coping with the rude demands of a dangerous world. Moreover, his cranial capacity was somewhat larger than that of his human equivalent. While a large brain is a prerequisite for superior intelligence, this does not in itself prove that Neanderthal man was superior in that regard to humans. But there is little doubt that our leading competitor, in the line of hominids, had mental ability at least as good as any, being a tool-maker with a material culture arguably not inferior to that of contemporary humans, and with a civilized capacity for burying his dead. Such burials even took place at a time when not all humans buried theirs. Some skeletons, especially those of children, must have had flowers put on their graves, for pollen has been found by microscopic detection. Neanderthals must have been a caring community, for skeletons exist of older members whose disabilities would have precluded them from being self-supporting. Why then did our own less powerful variety of hominid survive while our able and remote cousins perished in time?

Contrast then the robustness of our former contemporary with the basic anatomy of *Homo sapiens*. A specimen of our own kind hardly accords with the view of a being designed around the principle of Power. The skin is hairless, offering poor insulation properties. The teeth lack sharp incisors, the molars lack grinding power. The capacity for digesting food is restricted. Small nails in the hand suggest that former claws have lost their original function. The overall appearance portrays a delicate being, ill-fitted to withstand harsh conditions. Such a conclusion is in line with the results of occasional experiments in which humans are marooned in some remote location. There will be opportunities for living off the bounties of the wild. Nevertheless, after a short period of living rough in a desire to be self-supporting, the nature-lovers return in a sorry state, suffering from hunger and exposure. Intelligent, dedicated and supposedly educated people recurringly demonstrate their failure to master the problems of subsistence faced with the raw challenges of nature. Individual humans are not superbeings, like rats or goats which are capable of instantly adapting to and surviving in any environment they encounter.

Marooning an individual, it may be argued, is not a fair test of the basic capacity of a species. Individuals live in communities and communities provide social networks that operate to mutual advantage. So it seems likely that anatomical sacrifices would have been in order if these facilitated social interaction. A better understanding of this subject can be gained by taking a close look at those anatomical features that appear less functional than those of competitors. Is there due compensation for the loss of grinding strength of teeth and a weakening of the muscles of the mouth and throat that would inevitably limit the range of raw food that could be eaten? Here the anatomical data furnish clues. The notable variations relate to the shape and position of the basicranium, the mandible, the tongue, the epiglottis, the pharynx and the larynx. Operating in unison they create a wide range of sounds, more labial than nasal in nature and devoid of the barking quality that enables some mammals to transmit their messages over great distances. Arguably the only instance of the attempt to tackle communication at distance by physical means lies in yodelling, originally developed in mountainous regions for carrying simple messages across valleys. In general the human voice is better equipped for transmitting highly detailed messages over a *short* distance. Other hominids, whose skeletons have been studied, evidently possessed other types of voice-box. Here there are clues about how *Homo sapiens* differs from the last of our rival hominids. Computer studies have revealed that none was capable of producing vowels and ultimately sophisticated speech. So a new question arises. Why did sophisticated speech prove such a competitive advantage?

Before any conclusion can be reached and before the primaeval community can be reconstructed there are certain questions that need to be raised in relation to the body itself. Why does it appear so unsuited to protection against the elements? The thin skin is susceptible to rupture and abrasion, a potential hazard when wandering through thorny scrub. An even bigger disadvantage is the loss of insulation against temperature variations. While one must suppose that the smooth skin and bare body must have been adapted for warm rather than cold climates, very high temperatures would almost certainly have been experienced at times. So how would humans have coped? No doubt, just as they do now. In hot weather humans like to bathe. Therefore one must deduce that humans lived alongside riverbanks. Anatomically they were ideally designed to plunge into cooling rivers. Such a means of temperature regulation could also serve as a retreat and a protection against land predators, while, correspondingly, threats from water predators like crocodiles could be met by retreating onto land. Such suppositions about the ecology of the human species are in line with the evidence of the earliest remains being found in river valleys.

Yet the hairless skin possesses an additional form of biological utility that compensates for all its disadvantages and may have a more crucial bearing on how it arose in the first place. To understand its significance one needs to take account of how the reactions of the exposed skin, and the pores of the skin, impact on other functions of the body. The capacity of the human skin to sweat replaces the need for salivation as a means of regulating temperature, as is common among mammals generally. So the mouth, now exempted from this bodily duty, became free to further its specialized function in communication. But communication to what end? If any species is to survive and to thrive, it needs to achieve success in the fundamentals of existence which are quite limited in their range. They cover the reproduction of the species, the protection and raising of the young, the securing of food supplies and so ultimately the stability of the species itself. Any sustainable advance needs to operate in at least one of these areas. So what is the relationship between communication and reproduction or between communication and species stability?

The human method of reproduction is unusual (and indeed innovative) in several respects and therefore warrants analysis of its mysteries and meanings. Males do not mount females in mating, as in chimpanzees, but uniquely enter into sexual congress through a frontal body position. Here the mouth plays a key role in the preliminary stages and has distinguishing physical and functional characteristics. The lips of the mouth are much larger than any found in other mammals and are well furnished with sense organs, playing a notable part in the preliminaries of mating through that very unusual form of courtship called kissing. In the case of loquacious *Homo sapiens*, kissing can hardly occur without some words being spoken. The brevity of the spoken word can save fruitless physical effort. Women need not run away from advancing men without testing first their intentions. Words would signify rebuttal, just as they would physical enticement and acceptance. But a mouth can also construct a smile and a smile can lead to a kiss and set in motion a chain of distinctly human sexual responses. The mouth also plays a key part in establishing other forms of intimate communication at all stages of the life-span and even at the outset of life plays an important part in creating warm emotional attachments. Babies from the age of three months onwards smile and laugh in the same way among all peoples, even at the scheduled time in the case of babies born deaf–blind. By smiling, babies are programmed to delight adults and parents in partic-ular and so to receive the attention they need. Later the smiles of a pubescent will offer the first signs of encouragement to a member of the opposite sex and play a key part in flirting. Why does the mouth have such an important role to play in human behaviour? Whatever purposes the mouth has come to perform, primaeval man and primaeval woman must have been the first creatures to deliver vocal messages with precise meanings and without the necessity of gestures. A few words can set the scene in an economic, communal or sexual context.

Primaeval men and primaeval women have a few sexual features that are notably different from our closest relatives in the world (today) – chimpanzees – with whom we share ninety-eight per cent of our genes. The women of *Homo sapiens* menstruate in a way that makes them sexually available at all times, subject only to non-acceptance during a period. In other words, they have a relatively long *open season* and relatively short *closed season*.

Moreover, sexual availability is unrestricted by their season of fertility. In the rest of the animal kingdom, sexual availability *coincides* with the season of fertility, which occurs for a very limited period. The net effect is that there is a relatively short *open season* and a relatively long *closed season*. In the case of a number of mammals, the *open season* is so short that it may last for only two or three days in a year, as for example with foxes or pandas. An additional distinction is that sexual activity in humans is private and personal: in chimpanzees it is public. Females on heat are on offer to any passing male, although in practice the privilege is reserved for the dominant male.

While the human mating season is not limited by month or season, as it is with so many creatures, and can occur at any time of the year, greater sexual availability does not result in greater reproductive capacity. It is true that the production of semen from a sole male would be sufficient, if distributed with clinical precision, to sire and maintain the population of a medium sized country; the limiting factor, however, is woman's capacity to procreate. The rate of procreation will not exceed one child a year and the time-interval will be greater still if a mother is lactating. In summary, the balance between sexual activity and procreational outcome is the very reverse of being energy-effective. This can only mean that human sex is playing a role in survival that is *unrelated* to reproduction.

The apparent imbalance in reproductive capacity between male and female has been used to dispute the notion of pair-bonding as a fundamental human characteristic. For those attracted to the theory of the 'selfish gene', as advanced by Richard Dawkins, a view has been gaining ground that men are naturally polygamous while women are monogamous. In the greater biological interest of spreading their genes, it is alleged that men will seek every opportunity to implant their semen in women. In contrast, women need to be sure that they will have loyal mates if their children are to receive continued sustenance and protection. The interests of the two sexes diverge and are largely held together by cultural pressures.

While that argument has almost become part of the conventional wisdom, I do not think it can be sustained for two reasons. The first reason relates to the general principle of Evolution. The notion that men are polygamous and women monogamous is maladaptive in evolutionary terms. On *a priori* grounds the complementary nature of male and female sexual patterns would seem to have advantages over patterns that could be dysfunctional in a community. The second reason is that the facts do not lend support to the supposition. Men are not designed to serve a harem of women in the manner of stags (the historical prevalence of harems will be accounted for later in this book). The physical reality is that men can naturally deliver semen only when contained in a fluid called prostate which is limited in supply. Men cannot sustain repeated prostate production and loss as is demanded in a species of truly polygamous males. However boastful men may appear, the reality is that they are restricted in their sexual capacity in a way that women are not. A woman, who disregards her emotional inclinations, being motivated by money, or under external coercion, can enter into sexual congress with a number of men in continued succession. A similar feat on the part of men in relation to a comparable number of women can exist only in fantasy. The overall position then is that while women's greater sexual capacity is curtailed by their more focused preferences, men's more extended interests are curtailed by their sexual limitations. On this score the differing sexual characteristics of men and women, far from being at variance, appear complementary in operation, if not in character.

There are other biological phenomena that are distinctly human and therefore demand a functional explanation. The female menstrual cycle is a 'curse' to women and unwelcome to men. So does it serve a purpose? A related phenomenon adds to the mystery but also offers a clue. Young women living in close proximity tend to synchronize their menstrual cycles. It is believed the synchronization of female menstrual cycles is actuated by the production of pheromones to which a response is made by primitive pheromone-receptors. The whole process operates at a subconscious level. The inevitable consequence of group menstruation in a small community is to curtail sexual activity. In seeking an explanation of such a phenomenon, evolutionists have argued that collective menstruation is functional, since it prompts the exodus of the male hunting party. Its functional character gains further significance if account is taken of the lunar nature of menstruation. Menstruation, as the eponym implies, occurs once a month and, where it coincides, or can be induced to coincide, with the full moon, facilitates hunting at night when many animals are active. The functional interpretation of menstruation is that it promotes the departure of men on what may be termed community service. Such conjecture does not presume the simultaneous exodus of all the men within a community. Some young women will not menstruate because they have become pregnant or because they are due to give birth, so some men may decline to join the hunting party. Nor do they need to do so. Small hunting parties will almost certainly be more effective than large hunting parties and are least likely to disturb game. A possible overview therefore is that the function of group menstruation is to precipitate the departure of virile men in a hunting party of suitable size, while leaving behind a few old men or youths to give male protection and support to the community. By such an adaptive mechanism the range of the community's territory becomes effectively extended. In other words, regular expeditions compensate for any depletion of resources occurring when a community confines its activities and harvesting to its immediate neighbourhood. A hunting and gathering society is, in effect, a consumer society much like any other. Against the risk of a shortfall, supplies need to be regularly replenished.

So what other clues lead one to understand the functional significance of human sexuality? One unique physical feature of virgins is the existence of a hymen obstructing entrance to the vagina. Again, like menstruation, such a characteristic does not strike individuals as useful. The hymen is sore when broken and therefore acts as a disincentive to casual sexual activity. In other words, the hymen acts as a barrier to promiscuity at the outset of puberty, discouraging primaeval woman from accepting the sexual attentions of any passing male in the manner of female chimpanzees. Feminine responsiveness demands a proven sequence, comprising eye contact, words, kissing and touching, covering a much longer time-span. The existence of the hymen gives material support to the generality of monogamy and pair-bonding.

Strong incentives exist to maintain the pair-bond once established through sexual reinforcement. The anatomy of male and female genitalia furnishes a variety of supporting clues. Primatologists have drawn attention to the exceptionally large male phallus. Creatures of similar size and weight do not need such a relatively large organ in order to mate successfully. Indeed the disproportionate size of the phallus may account for why male nudity is often treated as shocking, whereas female nudity is treated as an art form. Disproportionality also arises in connection with the male testes, for these are far smaller than would be expected in other primates in relation to body weight. Large testes characterize chimpanzees and have a functional correspondence with their tendency to mate with all sexually available female chimpanzees. The restriction in the size of human testes testifies to a more restricted mating pattern as would befit pair-bonded relationships. In terms of the concepts of biological utility the size of the male phallus demands an explanation. The most likely is that the (undue) enlargement of the male sex organ serves to transmit pleasurable sensations. The size of the mammary glands is also reckoned to be far larger than the needs of lactation can justify and has been explained in terms of the part they play in male sexual arousal. Female genitalia, for their part, are also similarly enlarged, in comparison with other primates, but being internal are invisible. It is relevant that women possess a specialized, and largely hidden, sex organ called the clitoris containing a high concentration of sense endings. That organ is the only part of the human genitalia whose *sole* purpose is to generate sexual pleasure, performing no other discernible biologically useful function. The *hidden* feature of the clitoris corresponds with the *hidden* nature of female sexual behaviour.

At this point there is a seeming paradox that is central to an understanding of human sexuality. On the one hand, there are strong biologically rooted incentives to promote continuing human sexual activity. On the other hand, human sexual activity differs from that of other gregarious species by being private and restrained virtually to the point of secrecy. Women adorn themselves with cosmetics and decoration to heighten their sex appeal. But they do *not* decorate their genitalia. There is no counterpart to the heightened colouring of the female rump among chimpanzees. Even the reddening of the lips has been taken among humans as unduly provocative and is far from general in societies where women take a pride in being on display. While women may be keen to be noticed, traditional female behaviour is characterized by sexual modesty However, more subtle modes of communication become available once a mate is selected. There are clues here arising from those parts of the human body that are exempted from the uniformity of nakedness. That exemption is hair. Hair has forever been associated with women's charm and plays an important part in their self-awareness. To onlookers women will seemingly spend inordinate time in seeking to improve its appearance. But the more hidden hair may have even greater significance. The additional hair in both sexes is found surrounding the genitalia and under the armpits. The standard explanation is that such hair disperses sexually arousing scent. But this runs into two objections. The first is that far from being attractive, such odours are more inclined to repel a sexually interested party and prospective suitors are inclined to wash in the appropriate areas before attempting congress. The second objection is that most scantily clad aborigines prefer to cover their genitalia, which also looks contrary to the theory of continuous arousal. Such a custom implies that such sexual messages that can be conveyed are not there to be dispersed generally to all other members of the opposite sex but are restricted to a favoured partner. The positioning of hair at a level near to the nose certainly implies sexual signalling. The sweat glands under the armpits serve a general function in reducing body temperature by loss of water. But they also have a further part to play by acting as a dispersing agent. What they disperse are pheromones – aromatic compounds that convey subliminal chemical messages and have a very wide range of uses throughout the animal kingdom. So when two prospective mates are at close quarters, pheromones are exchanged. The message could be either be 'I am also attracted to you' or 'Actually, now you're close up, perhaps you're not my type after all'. The problem here is that if body odours are present from a different source, there will be interference with the message. This 'interference' factor needs closer examination. Possibly it was not a problem when the human form first evolved, for sweat is now known to be odourless. The odour stems from bacterial breakdown of the sweat and may have come about from a niche being created for the invasion of a specialized anaerobic bacterium as a result of the introduction of clothing. That bacterium has now been isolated and manufacturers of toiletries instead of masking it with perfume are addressing the challenge of its removal. Indeed, the perfume industry in the pursuits of its own interests has begun to revolutionize our understanding of human sexuality. That impetus is being furthered by the growing amount of research into human pheromones in American universities.

If the dispersion of pheromones is an important function of specialized sweat glands, the problem remains as to how these emissions are detected by humans. Only recently has a new perspective on this matter become possible by discovering the detector that corresponds to the producer of pheromones. That receptor is Jacobson's organ, a part of the nose that is chemo-receptive and serves to detect pheromones given off from human skin. This specialized area transmits signals to the hypothalamus, which controls the body's capacity for self-regulation and its ability to incorporate conditioned reflexes. In so doing, it bypasses consciousness. When people talk about the 'chemical attraction between people', there is in fact some literal truth in the popular notion. While the nose, in its broadest sense, is involved in this detection, Jacobson's organ is not strictly about smell, which relates to the olfactory glands, and relates to a distinctively different sense. Women are attracted (subliminally) to male pheromones and females (subliminally) to male pheromones. Studies carried out under experimental conditions show that both sexes move towards areas where the concentration of pher-omones of the other sex is most concentrated. Men can detect (subliminally) the pheromones of other men but the effect is to make them more aggressive either to each other or to an external group. Women, on the other hand, do not display any comparable aggressive response to the pheromones of other women. Perfume manufacturers have established that by adding male pheromones to perfumes women report feeling 'more secure'

The generally high rates of sexual liaison among humans appear to have no biological utility, being wasteful and running counter to the principle of the conservation of energy. The subordination of so many anatomical features, as discussed earlier, in the interest of maximizing sexual activity again appears to be uneconomic. Had procreation been the central focus of the evolutionary pattern, there would have been other, more efficient, ways of meeting that need. In place of wasteful sexual energy, there would have been more focused mating interest within a limited fertility period. The anatomical characteristics of pri-maeval woman might have been better designed for ease of childbirth. Not only is childbirth long, difficult, painful and dangerous for the mother, but the hazards result in a high level of infant mortality. A low rate of sexual activity and a high infant survival rate would have secured an equal or better rate of reproduction for the species than a high rate of sexual activity and a poor infant survival rate. It has been claimed that the distinctly human pattern of sexual activity serves the interests of the nuclear family by ensuring joint parental care during the long period of human infancy, childhood and learning. Pair-bonding in *Homo sapiens* may aid those activities. Yet pair-bonding is hardly essential in child-rearing, for in many native communities children are reared collectively. The loss of a male parent would scarcely have a disabling effect on the development of the primaeval infant. In any case male children in some tribes scarcely come within the purview of their fathers until they reach the age of puberty.

The only explanation I can venture, which takes account of all the anatomical and behavioural facts, is that the closeness of male and female relationships enabled a new type of community to evolve. It was a community that combined a gender-based division of labour with a common unity of purpose. Cross-gender communication was the key to its success. Through the avenue of sexual contact primaeval woman had access to an otherwise private male world. She had the means of expressing the needs of herself, her offspring and the community and she had the influence. For these two worlds of men and women to be co-ordinated language needed to flow across this gender gap. This is where women were well endowed. Primaeval men left to themselves tended to be laconic: words create noise and interfere with hunting. Even in the modern era men in their collective groupings pride themselves on the brevity of their language and wit. Women more usually among themselves prefer to chat and take their pleasure in conversation. Studies have shown that women write longer letters and have longer private telephone conversations. Women were well-fitted to become prime movers in developing cross-gender communication and the development of language in general. With a combination of communication and pyscho-sexual skills women developed an ability to control men. There are thus cogent reasons for concluding that Evolution hijacked the sex drive. It was refashioned to serve an ulterior purpose, an advantage that would benefit the species as a whole.

The view I have advanced on the basic importance of the male–female relationship for society does not necessitate that *all* of its members should fall into this pattern. In the context of primaeval society even a minority of such women operating along these lines could serve the communal purpose by representing the voice of others. The domestic needs of *one* primaeval woman would broadly resemble those of women in general. Prevailing on *one* primaeval man to bring back designated 'presents' on the hunting and gathering expedition would be transmitted to other members of a closely bonded male team. That is all that would be needed to ensure that men fulfilled their collective function as suppliers to women.

This rounded picture of how primaeval society functioned in general does not account for deviations in individual behaviour. There is a small but significant percentage of men and women

'If you bring me back an antelope haunch and a nice honeycomb, I'll mend your bearskin and have a nice meal waiting.'

who withdraw from normal sexual activities either through disinterest and asceticism or as a result of homosexual orientation. One cannot be sure whether such minorities existed in primaeval times or not and they do not seem to have been much in evidence in aboriginal communities, but elsewhere they have been found in all types of society. Their existence should not be presumed to operate against the interests of species survival. Take the case of genetically based homosexuals. In the context of desert communities, where expanding populations are not sustainable, homosexuality is often socially permitted. The diversion from reproductive activity can serve to protect the nuclear community from overpopulation and starvation. In these same areas, where at a later date polygamy became prevalent, the maldistribution of women would be liable to create tensions among men and generate conflict within the community. The emergence of male genetically based homosexuality would act as a safety valve and would therefore be biologically functional. Against that argument it can be contended that homosexuality would die out in a society out since homosexuals do not breed. The only feasible explanation for its continuation is that the genetic proclivity is transmitted through the female line. In communities when an alpha male secures a harem at the expense of other males, there is no biological utility in women giving birth to an oversupply of breeding males. However, I confess that here one is only at the stage of speculation and that further research is needed. Viewed pragmatically, a small percentage of homosexuals in a community creates no intrinsic problems. Individuals with cross-gender characteristics are able to undertake roles intermediate between those that are gender-typical. Diversity within a community provides a basis for spreading roles in social behaviour, so enlarging the resources on which the community and the species as a whole can draw in promoting its survival. The risk is that too much diversity will generate conflicts within the community or, even if these are contained, will result in wasted energies. Limited diversity can be contained within a society whose main body is functioning effectively.

These exceptions to the mainstream of human activities should not detract from the overall biological picture, which at this stage should be treated as a working hypothesis. It may be summed up as follows. Primaeval society can be reconstructed as pivoting on the core relationship between primaeval man and primaeval woman. To this end, Evolution made its overriding sacrifices in favour of the mouth as the key organ in communication and as the means of creating consensus. Communications across the gender division became the linkage point in creating social and economic order. The local domain of woman covered the need to care for the household and the children and to gather what was needed locally. The male orientation focused on a remoter domain, offering supplies of food and materials unavailable locally. The exploitation and co-ordination of these two domains offered an attractive evolutionary way forward.

Primaeval society may have been primitive in its beliefs, but the anatomical and biological evidence offers tentative support for the image (to be examined further in the next chapter) of a socially sophisticated and balanced society. Women were well furnished in body and temperament to act as the contractors and men as the suppliers. Women played a role at least as important as that played by men in contributing to the success of the community. By such natural arrangements the primaeval society predated any need for Power in sustaining the balance of its internal organization.

2

Echoes of the past

In the previous chapter I focused on the unique sexual anatomy of *Homo sapiens* and how its design facilitated pair-bonding. The continuity of male–female psycho-sexual relationships offered intimacy in communication and would facilitate the bridging and co-ordination of the otherwise separate domains of men and women. By affording the means of meeting overall community needs, it ensured the survival and continued progress of the species.

The use of sexuality to promote communication for communal advantage is rare among gregarious creatures. The only comparison that comes to mind relates to dolphins. Dolphins too are an intelligent and communicative species, with a strong sexual signalling system. Male and female contact involves stomach to stomach sexual positioning, beak to beak affinity (the closest to kissing), as with humans, plus a capacity for a high level of sexual availability operating over an extended time-span. Perhaps the human formula for using sexuality as the basis of social organization is not unique after all and its discovery was preempted by dolphins. If so, the formula may have a more general competitive advantage than has been previously acknowledged.

Without a doubt, the role of sexuality as the linchpin of the pair-bond has been largely ignored in the story of human evolution. If anything, the opposite standpoint has been fostered. Sexuality has been regarded as an 'animal' function from which humans have drawn apart by focusing on 'higher' and more spiritual activities. Sublimation is taken as the hallmark of civilization. There is even learned support for such a view from the writings of J.D. Unwin in *Sex and Culture*. His study of various levels of cultural development led him to a Freudian proposition that the *superego* can only advance by repressing the *id*. Great achievements demand the deferment of gratification, a condition allegedly absent in primitive peoples. If that viewpoint were upheld, it would be fair to claim that the evolutionary design of the human form was faulty and an impediment to progress. Instead of regarding sexuality as the linchpin of the pair-bond that holds human society together and therefore a highly *adaptive* function, a rival interpretation has arisen. Sexuality has been seen as 'lust' that diverts human society from creative endeavour and is therefore *maladaptive*. The second viewpoint is one that prevailed throughout several centuries of recent human history based on 'facts' that now need to be revisited. These 'facts' gained a particular boost once primitive peoples were 'discovered' by voyaging metropolitans. The intrinsic importance of gaining information about the subject lies in the possibility that existing hunter–gatherers are the *only* survivors of a type of society that existed many tens of thousands of years ago. Their observed patterns of behaviour could confirm or refute the conclusions reached on form and function in the previous chapter in respect of the basic design of human beings.

Historical documents indicate that so-called 'primitive' communities were traditionally believed to lack a moral sense and to be prone to promiscuity. This was the general opinion from the seventeenth century onwards, when explorers and traders first encountered sparsely clad natives possessing a limited material culture. The great voyages of exploration into the Pacific had brought to public attention islanders whose women had proved sexually available to visiting mariners. It was just such a situation that had brought about the mutiny on the *Bounty*, a ship engaged in the collection of samples of plants for purposes of serious scientific study and potential commercial exploitation. After the ship had called in at Tahiti the sailors decided that a better life could be had by rejecting the harsh conditions of life on board by offloading the Captain and his officers and returning to pick up pretty island girls and setting up a paradise isle. So it came about that they established a new community on the uninhabited island of Pitcairn. Sadly for them this operation soon lost its romantic glow as the seamen began killing one another in disputes over who should have which girls. After much bloodshed the emergent victors repented and reverted to the norms of civilization by becoming pious Christians. It was not the only famed event to which the island gave rise. The notion that free love was available in Tahiti (the island from which the women of Pitcairn had been snatched) percolated back to France, its colonial masters. Such a beckoning opportunity accounted for the decision of Gauguin to set up home there, a decision commemorated in many of the most famous works of the artist. These paintings, with their bare-breasted women, helped to confirm and proclaim to a largely prudish public the view that native women with their brazen lack of modesty lacked the sexual morality of their civilized counterparts.

Contemporary encounters with hitherto undiscovered humans were also taking place in previously unexplored continents. During the eighteenth century the British, French, Belgian, German, Dutch, Spanish and Portuguese took full advantage of their superiority in weaponry to annexe great swathes of territory in many parts of the globe. Inevitably these creators of empire clashed with one another. Yet by the end of the nineteenth century the leading colonial powers reached a measure of agreement as to how undeveloped parts of the world were to be divided and shared between them. Lines would be drawn across maps with a ruler. All the territory on one side of the line would belong to one colonial power and all the territory on the other side to another. Once that settlement had been reached, each occupying colonial power was now free to exploit its acquisition and soon set about despatching, or agreeing to license, expeditions into the interior in the search for exotic materials and potential sources of wealth. Freed from the risk of challenge from any other colonial power, the only source of opposition now came from the natives. Of course these were not party to any agreement about the annexation of their territories. Most tribal people did not think in terms of *owning* territory about which they were in a position to negotiate. Nor in any case did the many tribes who occupied a large expanse of territory belong to any larger political entity so they could scarcely have entered into any such discussion even if it had been on offer. As far as they were concerned the presence of strange faces only conveyed the message that their territory was being invaded. Skirmishes inevitably resulted. Of course spears and arrows proved no match for rifles and cannon. Yet since fierce resistance had been encountered, the natives were regarded as savages. The term was soon applied to all the denizens of a primitive material culture, even by that gifted chronicler of primitive superstition and religion, Sir James Frazer, in his voluminous work *The Golden Bough*, published in 1913.

The victorious colonizers soon consolidated their hold on these vast new territories. While hazards in moving into them still remained, small expeditions could now be mounted into the interior. But their prospects of success much depended on how far the natives could be won over and porters recruited. While force could always be held in reserve much was achieved by offering 'presents', sometimes little more than trinkets. Once co-operation had been secured, a few intrepid explorers with only limited resources could successfully make their way over vast tracts of territory into areas that had never before seen a European. The information brought back from these explorations often made sensational reading for wide-eyed city-dwellers. It was found that in a 'friendly' tribal area hospitality offered by a chieftain might include the offer of a young girl for the night. Titillating details would be reported about the temptations awaiting explorers given overnight accommodation in a native hut. As might be expected, the story would always conclude on a sober note. The chronicler would be keen to affirm that virtue, as befitted someone with a Christian upbringing, had been duly maintained. Such reports could scarcely fail to impart a general lesson. Herein lay the proof of the contrast between 'moral' Europeans and 'immoral' natives. It was no less a shock to readers residing in a wholly monogamous culture to learn that native chieftains could have many wives, an entitlement, it seemed, that was conferred by wealth and position. Was it such loose and immoral behaviour that accounted for the backwardness of the natives? In the prevailing view of the times there was no doubt about the answer. So it was conceived as the duty of the civilizing powers to send out missionaries to convert the natives, to teach them about sin and to ensure they were properly clothed.

And yet that era of discovery also triggered a significant and new interest in native peoples: it stemmed from the progress of science culminating in an event that had rocked society to its foundations. The theory of evolution had proposed that humans were descended from apes. If our ancestors were ape-men, modern humans were perhaps closer to 'savages' than had been realized. For fertile minds one question now became uppermost: could further study help humans to understand their origins? So the spirit of the times gave rise to a new academic subject – *anthropology*, focusing on the habits and beliefs of primitive peoples. University Faculties now engaged in a determined search to find suitable material for this newly emerging subject. Only in this way could the subject gain the academic standing that universities demanded. Accordingly, research workers were appointed and duly despatched to live among selected tribes. There they sought to gain the confidence and intimacy of those they were studying without disturbing the strictly objective nature of their assignments. Anthropologists were there strictly to observe and record and certainly not to indulge in any amenities that might be forthcoming from native girls. Nor did it appear that such amenities were on offer. Isolated tribes had a strong culture of their own which, the evidence suggested, seemed the more complex the more it was studied. The initiative proved justified. Patterns of behaviour were observed that had never previously been recorded and contrasted sharply with the travellers' tales of the early explorers. Anthropologists became the first to appreciate that a line of distinction needed to be drawn between true aborigines and those tribes-people whose fragile cultures had been affected by earlier visitors or disturbed by invaders, or who had installed themselves as conquerors of the former occupants of the territory.

In due course it became clear that the first barely clad peoples reported by early explorers had already been 'discovered' by others. Their culture bore all the traces of culture contamination. The islanders had been visited on earlier occasions by passing ships and there was little doubt that European venereal diseases had been imported. On the subject of foreign influences, many of the locations of the African hinterland, first visited by and sensationally reported on by European explorers, had already been worked over by slave-traders. Supplying people as slaves had become an acknowledged business. The claimants of a 'discovery' often need to be treated with reservation, for they usually lack the historical background or knowledge to justify their claims. Did Christopher Columbus, setting out on a mission to open up a new route to India, really 'discover' America? Instead, 'The first to publicize the existence of' might have been a better description of the reality.

There was, however, one compelling reason for a full investigation into the nature and culture of primitive peoples. The newly acquired colonial territories needed to be administered. The largest of the empires in the heyday of colonialism was the British Empire, so global and extensive that it was termed the empire on which the sun never set. Government service within this vast empire was a prestige appointment and its recruits were customarily drawn from the most favoured universities. Faculties of Anthropology were duly set up at Oxford and Cambridge with the implicit purpose of gaining a basic understanding of these new colonial people. Those who graduated from these Faculties were judged the most appropriate people to become colonial administrators. Appointed as District Commissioners, they proved sympathetic towards the tribal peoples they had studied and took professional pride in recording their experiences.

This new subject established a few basic points that can serve as background to our further inquiry. Archetypal tribal people live in small communities. Those that farm use extensive rather than intensive farming techniques, relying on shifting agriculture (characterized by 'slash and burn'), and engage in nomadic or semi-nomadic livestock herding or live wholly or partly on wild produce, gathering plants, hunting and fishing. The economic self-sufficiency of these tribal people distinguishes them from peasants, who depend to some limited extent on the market economy. More numerous are those whose culture is partly 'tribal' but who are none the less detribalized. Many people in the territories of empire had lost their tribal organization and economy through their contacts with industrial civilization and were not therefore typical of anything.

The preference of anthropologists to find and study *genuinely* tribal and primitive people was governed to some extent by the needs of academic stringency. It was important that the phenomena reported from their studies could not be attributed to extraneous variables. Such studies needed to be as 'pure' as possible. Primitive cultures are fragile and easily disturbed by intrusive outsiders. Once overwhelmed, they take on many characteristics, and often the worst, of the intruders. As a consequence, many *hybrid* native communities display a whole range of behaviours that move them away from their origins and are more like those that characterize (one might even say afflict) modern or mediaeval societies.

The significance of these pioneering anthropologists is that they succeeded in uncovering data that were very near to vanishing forever. Whatever their original purpose might have been, the information they compiled served ultimately to offer clues for understanding the behavioural roots of humans as a species. So if the human form evolved as a refined adjustment to the ecosystems prevailing at least fifty thousand or a hundred thousand years ago, it is only fitting that search should be made for any representatives of this prehistoric era who could have survived in the world today. The current position is that very small pockets of aboriginal people, indigenous to the territories they inhabit, are still to be found living in remote locations. Introduced diseases from which they have no immunity, the effects of logging and the general destruction of their environment have greatly reduced their numbers. Indeed, the ultimate but sad jest of the modern world is that aborigines may be defined as any small group of natives surrounded by a large number of anthropologists. But a century ago, when anthropological studies were flourishing, it was a very different matter. Adequate numbers of simple tribal people allowed much field material to be collected and analysed. That material, well-documented and safely stored today in libraries, remains a great human treasure-trove, forever waiting to be re-analysed and re-evaluated.

The central issue from the point of view of our inquiry is how far these aboriginal people furnish important clues as to the nature of the primaeval community. Are they the true descendants, retaining their original characteristics? By remaining true to type have they paid a heavy price? Have they suffered the misfortune of being pushed into less than habitable regions by more aggressive and sophisticated neighbours? If so, they deserve the reverence and sympathy of their distant modern relatives. Indeed they should be valued, for these survivors could retain for humanity lessons that have been largely lost from human corporate memory. Or should one accept the counter-argument, which is that aboriginal people should be viewed as 'losers' in the struggle to come to terms with a developing world?

If so, such 'failures' could scarcely serve as representative of a previously thriving primaeval culture and should not therefore be taken as offering a window on the past. Yet in their 'failure' there lies an element of success. By retaining their identity in spite of huge external pressures that forced them into scarcely habitable terrain, these aboriginal peoples have testified to their inner strengths. Surviving under the most adverse conditions, they have been pushed into harsh environments that other peoples did not care to occupy. And yet they have held to their culture often more firmly than more sophisticated peoples have succeeded in retaining theirs. Their conservatism serves as a distant echo of the past. On balance, there seems a strong case for believing that aboriginal communities are similar or even very similar to primaeval communities that existed many thousands of years ago. If therefore one is to search for the original model of the human being, the study of aborigines offers a rich source of material.

At this juncture I must clarify the terminology I intend to use about our target group. *Aborigines* will refer to all those small pockets of fully tribal and self supporting people who live, or who did live during the period when they were studied, in climatically harsh and largely impenetrable regions. This choice of definition will mean dropping alternative terms – 'savages' or natives or tribal people or primitive people. About these discarded terms, the first seems too insulting, the second too indefinite and the third too general. The fourth seems not only too condescending but also presupposes that lack of material development correlates with social and political simplicity. Of the large body of general observational material accumulated by anthropologists, it is clear that some important distinctions need to be made. For the purpose of tracing human evolution a line needs to be drawn between *aboriginal* material and material pertaining to *invader* tribes who have taken territory from the indigenous population. Aboriginal material has a distinctive character about it. Its special feature relates to an immensely complex kinship system. The vocabulary for describing blood relationships far exceeds any that exists in the vocabulary of modern languages. Even without written language aborigines can sometimes trace kinship patterns through ten or eleven generations. Permitted marriage patterns operate for the most part as though constructed on biological grounds in order to exclude inbreeding. Such exogamy in the case of jungle aborigines reaches the point where wives are customarily taken from another tribe with the consequence that husband and wife do not share a common language. Yet that exchange provides a further advantage that each tribe will contain interpreters who can have a useful part to play in local trading or communal negotiation. Such care and elaboration in these and other types of exogamous practices refute the notion of sexual licentiousness and immorality. The contrary picture is far better supported. Aboriginal communities are revealed as highly moral, with elaborate notions of obligations towards one another; giving and sharing are the norms among those who are blood relatives. Additionally, adjacent communities have a common interest in retaining friendly ties and relationships.

Aboriginal communities are notable for the status conferred on women. Women display 'freedom in their behaviour allied with dignity'. Such an observation is further supported by the structural nature of aboriginal society. It is not unusual to find their cultures characterized by the matrilineal tracing of descent. The mother is the reference point of the clan. In the raising of children the leading male role is sometimes played by the mother's brother. Such a pattern contrasts with contemporary society where genealogy presents patrilineal patterns of kinship, as though genes were passed entirely through the male line. The explanation in aboriginal society, as anthropologists discovered, was that not all communities associated sex with reproduction. If all women who reach puberty enter into sexual activity (being the boon of pleasure that Nature offered), the fact that they give birth was associated with the magical properties of being a woman rather than with sex itself. There was no logical need to see sex as a necessary part of the process. With that background in thinking, ancestry and kinship became a predominantly female subject. Women were revered for their ability to give life.

Kin, being traced along the female line, is compatible with matrilocal marriage, defined as the condition in matrimony whereby a husband goes to live with his wife's group. Such social practice casts women in a leading role that has no fitting parallel in history, where patriarchy has predominated. The degree of this inversion has given rise to notions of its direct opposite – *matriarchy*. The term is sometimes employed to describe those modern, usually working-class, families where the wife receives her husband's pay packet, controls the household budget, after passing on money for beer and cigarettes, and generally makes all the decisions for the family. The concept of matriarchy has also been raised speculatively as possibly underlying the primaeval community. The oldest artefacts, dating some tens of thousands of years ago, comprise fecund female figures. It is supposed that these served as fertility objects in a belief that their presence would improve crops. But as the givers of life, there is a theory that sees women as possessing greater powers than men. Here it is noteworthy that many of the oldest recorded gods were female. If primaeval society was not a patriarchy, could its antithesis have been the prevailing pattern? Could the prominence of women, confirmed by matrilineal and matrilocal survivals, point to a matriarchal society as being the norm in the deepest and fast-fading past of human society?

I am bound to say that none of the anthropological studies of which I am aware have reported such a phenomenon among aborigines. The fact that communities are *not* patriarchal should not be taken to denote the converse – that they are in reality matriarchal. It is quite conceivable that within a household a woman may display indisputably matriarchal behaviour. This she is entitled to do since she is operating *within* her domain. But matriarchal behaviour in the all-gender collective unit would mean operating *beyond* her domain. In aboriginal societies significant decisions need to be taken from time to time that affect the whole community. This does not mean that one sex necessarily dominates another. In practice, anthropologists report that decision-making is not confined to a single gender but arises through consensus. Aboriginal societies are communicating societies. Through involving all members of the community in the processes that customs allow, commitment is secured for any decision that is reached. Aboriginal communities cannot be properly dubbed either patriarchal or matriarchal. The absence of this type of gender dominance or of formal hierarchy raises the general question of what alternative means exist for communal decision-making.

In giving this subject closer scrutiny account needs to be taken of one major structural problem. A notable feature of aboriginal society is the absolute nature of the gender-related division of roles. Hunting and fishing are exclusively male occupations, as are the making of tools and weapons. Women prepare food and make clothes and gather anything the community may need, including water, from the environs of the settlement. The roles never overlap except under conditions of stress when there may be temporary aberrations from the settled pattern. Even when older men can no longer join with others in the hunt and are largely confined to sedentary activities, they do not engage in the roles of women but take on older male roles, repairing fishing nets or broken tools. The roles of men and women are so sharply differentiated that they often employ different vocabularies. There are words that women will use that men will never use and vice versa and there are different forms of common words according to the gender of the person speaking. In this respect there are similarities with many modern languages where male and female (and neutral) genders of nouns have survived and serve as testimony to the archetypal nature of the gender-based division of language and of roles. Yet there are also words that have no gender-linkage and are used equally freely by men and women.

If in aboriginal communities the life-patterns of men and women are so sharply differentiated, if women are revered and if decisions are made by consensus rather than by any single-gender group, then a problem presents itself. By what means could a society modelled on such lines achieve any form of coherence and consensus? In the context of a modern group such a pattern would be deemed 'shambolic'. People would see matters from different viewpoints and there would be no agreement.

In the case of aboriginal society that difficulty is much reduced by the unifying effect of religion. Religion in this context encompasses a set of beliefs, concerns and compulsions that cover every aspect of life and are shared equally by all members of the community. Such beliefs start with the origins of the tribe, how they came into this world and what binds them together. The world is seen as an interacting whole. All material beings have a spiritual counterpart. The dream world, which figures so prominently in Australian aboriginal society, is also part of the living world. The departed spirits of ancestors need to be nurtured. They must never be forgotten for it is by remembering that they are kept alive. The birds and beasts embody particular virtues and cannot be exploited without the need for propitiation. Even the vegetable world can contain spirits. This may entail, as Frazer so famously recorded, apologizing and propitiating the spirit of a tree before it is felled, so allowing the tree-spirit to escape.

Managing community in the best possible way requires an association with good spirits by physical means and even consuming spirits contained within the flesh while fending off the bad by magical devices. Cannibalism was practised in widely separated parts of the world, where humans possessed some much admired quality. Anything holy, or deemed a source of wonder, would be liable to be eaten, for by that means higher powers would be ingested by the eater. Many of the practices of aborigines might appear barbaric to the modern mind. They may have been misguided but in their setting they were expressing awe in a physical form for the deceased. All relationships are founded on a universal value, which may be termed Respect. Aborigines have always shown Respect for Nature. Respect for all living things would cover both bird and beast. Men would show Respect for the rights of women, just as women would

'Sorry tree-spirit. I'll give you a couple of minutes to get out.'

show Respect for the rights of men, and neither gender would emulate the other. Yet these deferential rights were not seen as personal entitlements but as collectively demanded practices: they belonged to the community and were part of Nature. Drought, typhoon, flood and plague would be Nature's response to the violation of Her laws. An uncle who made sexual advances to his niece might offend propriety. But the more serious aspect of the offence would be to put at risk the well-being of the community. Elaborate rituals would be needed, involving some humiliation on the part of the offender. Conspicuous group punishment was necessary if the evil consequences of the offence were to be averted.

The regulating pattern of aboriginal society pivoted on totems and taboos. The totem symbolizes a spirit. As an emblem, in the form of an animal or bird, it conveys those qualities it represents to whomsoever wears its insignia as decorations or articles of clothing. The physical existence of the totem serves to fix an otherwise fleeting, abstract idea. The totem is as important as the cultivation of ancestor-spirits in acting as a reminder of community values. While totems give expression to the ideals binding the society together, those ideals need to be counterbalanced by the existence of prohibitive boundaries. This is where a Polynesian word, now incorporated into the English language, expresses the boundary markings through the rules of *taboo*. Taboos in practice take the form of forbidden behaviours or words, violation of which triggers peril. For example, aboriginal tribes in many parts of the world avoid mentioning the name of an immediate relative or an ancestor. It is not that those names are altogether private, since they are used by others who are not in the same relationship. The standing of permissible and impermissible names will vary according to tribe. To the outsider the way in which these name conventions operate might appear almost arbitrary and inexplicable. But Frazer's study of hundreds of these taboos shows an underlying pattern. Name taboos are more likely to apply to those in a very *close* relationship, as in the case of husband and wife. Elaborate circumlocutions are then needed to enable the listener to understand to whom the speaker is referring. Rather than use the name the speaker will use a pun on the name or mention an animal with qualities as a totem that will indicate the identity of the person. The real motive behind the name taboo is to offer protection to the spirit of a loved one. Mention of a forbidden name exposes the individual to danger since the word becomes an entry to the soul and may be likened to a source of infection. Similarly, standing on a person's shadow is often taboo, for the soul is thereby diminished. Many writers at the time when these phenomena were first reported named fear as the primary emotion explaining taboos. However, others who have studied aborigines point out that descriptions of fears do not figure prominently in aboriginal stories. Taboos play an important part in regulating aboriginal society and need to be understood in relation to a wider context. Aboriginal taboos to a great extent hinge on respect for spirits and highlight the sensitivity of such communities towards personal relationships and relationships with the natural world with which the community is so closely embroiled.

Not all taboos can be explained in this way. Some, like incest, are so widespread as to apply to modern and aboriginal communities alike. They give the impression of being biologically rooted, for they do not need to be learned or taught. However, rather than focus on the origin of all the taboos, it is more important to heed their function. Here one can take account of an anthropological school of thought called *functionalism*. This school maintains that the beliefs and customs of primitive communities operate in a way that promotes coherent functioning in that society. Taboos act as regulators, socializing conventions, cementing relationships and building up mutual expectations. They serve to prevent members of the community from over-stepping the mark. Totems and taboos provide the framework of a moral society free from the needs of enforcement for its organizational effectiveness. The cogency is supplied by belief. Aboriginal beliefs fall into two main categories. There are beliefs that explain, or attempt to explain the origins of the tribe, the roots of creation, or how particular animals acquired their idiosyncratic characteristics. Since such beliefs look backwards into the past, they neither facilitate nor impede the way in which society functions. But beliefs about the present, along with the credence given to the powers of magic, are potentially maladaptive. Beliefs that are illusions obstruct progress, obscuring the relationship between cause and effect. They therefore present problems of how aboriginal society can manage itself without becoming victims of its own beliefs. But before that question is tackled, more needs to be said about the dynamic nature of those beliefs if one is to understand how the human mind operated in its first edition.

Frazer considered beliefs in magic fell into two types; there was sympathetic magic and contagious magic. Sympathetic magic operates in the supposition that a parallel activity will have an influence on another activity. For example, a woman engaged in a difficult labour can be assisted by a husband who himself goes into labour, a practice so widespread that it bears a defining name – the *couvade*. Reciprocally, wives can help their husbands when they are at sea by avoiding anything that could contribute to a rough sea, like pounding grain or chopping wood. Another method for safeguarding those on a voyage would be for three or four young girls, specially chosen for the duty, to remain in one room with their hands clasped between their knees. They should not turn their heads to left or right, for if they did it would cause the boat to pitch and toss. By remaining motionless for as long as possible, calm water would be assured.

People can influence crops while to an equivalent extent the crops can influence people. A pregnant woman sitting beneath a tree will encourage that tree to bear fruit. On the other hand, a barren wife should avoid getting close to fruiting trees for fear that as a consequence the tree will fail to fruit. When it comes to planting, the length of the hair can be important. Women with long hair will promote the growth of long stalks in rice and in maize. Maize also benefits from being planted by people with a good set of even teeth, for otherwise there will be empty spaces in the maize cob corresponding to the empty spaces in the planter's teeth. Another sympathetic device for assisting crops to grow relies on leaping and dancing before or after sowing. The higher the leaping, the higher the crops will grow.

The prevalence of sympathetic magic in aboriginal communities carries an eloquent message about how such people feel. Sympathetic magic, as the name implies, appeals to people who are especially 'sympathetic' and approach their whole environment with a sense of empathy. That environment includes both people and plants. The mutual nature of that relationship between plants is illustrated by a practice presumed by its practitioners to have educational value. Frazer recounts it as follows (p. 144):

> *To improve a child's memory the Cherokees beat up burs in water fetched from a roaring waterfall. The virtue of the potion is threefold. The voice of the Long Man or river-god is heard in the roar of the cataract; the stream holds things cast upon its*

surface; and there is nothing that sticks like a bur. Hence it seems clear that with the potion the child will drink in the lessons taught by the voice of the waters, will seize them like the stream, and stick fast to them like a bur.

Another useful practice where humans are in need of restoration has been cited from the choice of fuel for the cooking of food. The beneficiary would need to (p. 145):

eat food cooked on a fire which was fed by wood which had grown out of the stump of a tree which had been cut down. The recuperative power manifested by such a tree would in due course be communicated through the wood to the fire . . . and so to the person who ate the food which was cooked on the fire which was fed with the wood which grew out of the tree.

Sympathetic magic works through telepathic transmission on the supposition through simulation that the sender and the recipient are put into spiritual communication with one another. Contagious magic, on the other hand, works by contact rather than by resemblance.*

* Sir James Frazer, *The Golden Bough*, Part One, vol. 1, p. 175, first edition 1913, reprinted Macmillan 1990):

> *The most familiar example of Contagious Magic is the magical sympathy which is supposed to exist between a man and any severed portion of his person, as his hair or nails; so that whoever gets possession of human hair or nails may work his will, at any distance, upon the person from whom they were cut. This superstition is world-wide; instances of it in regard to hair and nails will be noticed later on in this work.[1] While like other superstitions it has had its absurd and mischievous consequences, it has nevertheless indirectly done much good by furnishing savages with strong, though irrational, motives for observing rules of cleanliness which they might never have adopted on rational grounds. How the superstition has produced this salutary effect will appear from a single instance, which I will give in the words of an experienced observer. Amongst the natives of the Gazelle Peninsula in New Britain 'it is as a rule necessary for the efficiency of a charm that it should contain a part of the person who is to be enchanted (for example, his hair), or a piece of his clothing, or something that stands in some relation to him, such as his excrements, the refuse of his food, his spittle, his footprints, etc. All such objects can be employed as* panait, *that is, as a medium for a* papait *or charm, consisting of an incantation or murmuring of a certain formula, together with the blowing into the air of some burnt lime which is held in the hand. It need hardly, therefore, be said that the native removes all such objects as well as he can. Thus the cleanliness which is usual in the houses and consists in sweeping the floor carefully every day, is by no means based on a desire for cleanliness and neatness in themselves, but purely on the effort to put out of the way anything that might serve an ill-wisher as a charm.'[2]*

1 Meantime I refer the reader to *The Golden Bough*, Second Edition, L 367 *sqq.*
2 R. Parkinson, *Dreissig Jähra in der Südsee* (Stuttgart, 1907), pp. 118 *sq.*

A belief in contagious magic has been considered to have a beneficial effect on hygiene. The huts of aborigines are often kept scrupulously clean lest some physical particle of its inhabitant might fall into the wrong hands, so allowing an evil spell to transfer itself on to the person. Magic can therefore have a functional purpose.

While magic is designed to influence fate, it is not irreversible. Here again contagious magic has a role to play. The experience is quoted of an expedition of missionaries in a jungle in the Celebes when one of their porters heard a cry of a certain bird. Its warning signified that if a further step forward was taken disaster would befall the party. The missionaries declined to heed the warning. One of the porters then devised a solution. Hair taken from one of the party was placed in a special spot and covered with a shroud of sticks and leaves. In that way the spell was transferred from the party to the hair, so allowing the party to proceed with impunity.

If taboos are ignored they spell misfortune. But there are many occasions when it becomes necessary for their outcomes to be averted. Here to the rescue comes the shaman. The word shaman originated in eastern Siberia, meaning 'one who is excited or raised'. Throughout the hunter–gather world community-based ritual specialists heal the sick and provide spiritual protection. They mediate between the social/human world and the dangerous and unpredictable world of the supernatural. Shamanism emphasizes performance, mixing theatre and instrumental acts as the avenue of approach to the sacred.

The shaman has a variety of equally magical remedies or spells that allows him or her to overcome the inevitable. Should that remedy fail, the inevitability of ill fortune that follows the breaking of the taboo is confirmed. However, should the remedy succeed, trust is strengthened in the powers of the shaman. Either way people are reassured. The system of all-pervasive magic has a built-in stability that assures its continuation while also offering a degree of adaptation.

The evidence from a great range of anthropological studies poses a question that suggests a paradox. On the one hand, aboriginal societies display a remarkable sophistication in terms of how they operate as a community, managing their affairs without resort to single-person power. Respect for one another, for the community and for nature allow them to live in harmony with their environment. Further, the testimony of adventurers who have travelled with aborigines across semi-desert savannahs or through jungles bears out their remarkable capacity for understanding the forces of nature and knowing how to cope with them. The results speak for themselves. In spite of formidable challenges from their demanding environments aborigines are typically well fed and enjoy good health during their relatively short span of life. On the other hand, the beliefs of these socially sophisticated communities are truly and recurringly primitive. Association-thinking acts as a barrier to rational thought and on the face of it would consign such communities to everlasting backwardness. If aboriginal communities are indeed echoes of the primaeval community from which all humans are descended, can one explain how progress and invention have arisen from a background of primitive thought?

The possible answer to that puzzle lies in two safeguards which can ensure vitality in seemingly primitive communities. The first safeguard is that dynamic spells and practices are always on hand to avert unwanted outcomes, and they spring from a set of 'reserve' beliefs. Such belief-systems contrast with more contemporary exclusive religious and political doctrines which are binding and inflexible. The magic-man or shaman will find a way out of the crisis by summoning a new counter-force or spell in response to perceived needs. There is nothing that is done that cannot be undone. The second safeguard lies in the escape-route from old beliefs which arises where new challenges create new scenarios. Where there is no challenge, the ever-active human mind invents causes and effects and in a static environment becomes victim of its own projections. The myths then become forces in their own right. But where there is challenge, human endeavours can be judged by results that can be perceived. Then experience plays a greater role in formulating beliefs and theories and punishes misconceptions or misapplications. And so a divide ultimately opens up between pragmatism and mythology.

The mass of aboriginal societies of which we possess recorded evidence have been hemmed into particular terrains, not because they were conducive to human habitation but because their migration to better locations has been debarred by existing occupants. Incarcerated in inhospitable lands aborigines have looked inwards rather than outwards and so have developed conservative life-styles. The need to wrestle with unfamiliar challenges has been rendered unnecessary by regularities of their existence.

Herein then lies a possible difference between the original primaeval community (and our direct descendants) and those residual bands of aborigines that survive today or have been recorded in their greater numbers in earlier centuries. One hundred thousand years ago primaeval communities were not hemmed in by rival populations, as aborigines are today. The human anatomy was perfectly adapted to the habitat in which humans had sprung given those social practices to which primaeval men and women were predisposed. In the first chapter of this book primaeval society was reconstructed, at least theoretically, by taking the approach of psychobiology. Tentative conclusions were reached that have been put into store. This chapter has acted as a cross-check on those conclusions by seeking evidence from a rapidly vanishing human world. One cannot be sure whether aboriginal communities may be likened to human museums, thereby preserving the ways of the remote past and echoing its theme and styles of living. There are, however, parallels between the customs and practices of aborigines, so obviously different in thoughts and customs from modern humans, and what can be presumed about the social and political dimensions of the primaeval age on the basis of psychobiology. The two pictures, approached from different angles, present a coherent whole.

So now the story of human evolution needs to move on. A new era was about to open for mankind. What conditions brought about the mass exodus from Paradise? What new forces changed the direction of Evolution and gave rise to a different variety of human being?

3

The Great Migration

For every species of the living world that functions as a family or group a relationship exists between size of population and territory. Populations remain relatively stable in numbers within a territory. Since population and territory are kept in balance territory will be defended vigorously against intruders. Should a given population increase by natural means, instability will set in. The most painless solution is for part of the community to hive off from the parent body, to migrate to a new territory and to form a new community. By this self-adjusting process the parent community is restored to numbers corresponding to its ideal size. Successful and expanding species ultimately demand the penetration of new territories. Then new problems arise, for the ecosystem may differ in a number of respects from the territory that has been quitted. A species with specialist habits and requirements that leaves its territory may fail to adapt to the challenges of the new environment and is likely to perish. The most successful colonists are species that have developed a range of behaviours and are able to live off the possibly unfamiliar sources of food supply that the new environment offers.

Against that background one can consider the challenge that eventually faced primaeval humans. Our ancestor, the naked ape, was clearly best adapted in physical design to inhabiting the localities of river courses in a warm climate. River beds would provide a source of stones which could be used as tools and the water would enable food and materials to be washed. The naked body could be protected from overheating by bathing in the river. The river could also act as a refuge from savage four-legged beasts. By retreating into the river mothers would offer security to their young. Rivers would offer or be close to a supply of good drinking water, an essential requirement for humans prone to sweat profusely from the large area of their exposed flesh. The river had the additional advantage that it could offer fish as a potential food supply to supplement the fruits of the forest or savannah. The river was the ideal environment for *Homo sapiens* as designed by the long and complex processes of evolution. It is scarcely surprising that even today humans feel most relaxed when they are reclining in the sun close by water.

But Paradise for humans did not last forever. Whether due to climatic change or over-population, small colonies needed to move away from their parent body into an adjacent environment. In the case of early humans contact was kept and indeed consolidated through the practice of exogamy (that is, marrying someone from an external group). Hence through inter-marriage the biological faults that flow from in-breeding were avoided. Communities became better spaced, the balance in the ecosystem was restored, and the stock of *Homo sapiens* was improved and maintained within the ecosystem, all at the same time.

But in due course the situation became unstable once the accessible habitats became fully populated. In Nature such a scenario gives rise to combat between groups for limited territory with the result that one group wins and drives out the other. The stock of the winning group increases while the stock of the losing group falls. In this context the survival of the fittest relates to the group as a whole, so offering an evolutionary advantage for the species itself. Another mode of self-regulation arising from over-crowding is for increased stress levels to have an inhibiting effect on breeding levels. The breeding rate then falls allowing the balance to be maintained in the density of population within the traditional territory. These common solutions in Nature were not so readily available for humans. Humans without weapons are not well equipped for fighting and by their archetypal nature, as a co-operating community, were not disposed to contest territories through competitive struggles and warfare with other groups.

When humans decided to abandon their original habitat and sought to find another, they were well placed to take advantage of their triple strengths – their learning ability, capacity for teamwork and a rudimentary division of labour. Instead of restricting their breeding, as commonly happens in the animal kingdom through competition between males, humans spread out from the favoured river beds and moved inland into a more arid environment. There the ever-pressing need to find water could be overcome by following herds that depended on and could detect water holes. New hunting skills developed and eating habits changed. The disposition of men to explore, combined with the resourcefulness of women in making best use of what the men found, helped to make viable what otherwise would have been a barely marginal strategy. The true measure of a successful species lies in its ability to subsist in an environment different from that in which it originated. It is here that humans fared well. A move from a climatically ideal environment would not have been feasible without clothing, which adept human hands were well equipped to supply, though at first in a primitive way. The division of labour rather than being modified was now intensified as the development, design and making of clothes became the exclusive prerogative of women. It is easy to envisage the scene as the skins of animals brought back as meat initiated a new gender-related enterprise with a new use being found for what would otherwise have been waste material. In turn, the concept of clothing hugely extended the range of humans and allowed them to move into new types of habitat. Some continued as migrating hunters, others discovered the amenities of caves, the cool and deep interiors of which provided long-term storage of meat supplies and security against scavengers, and in such sanctuaries they established settlements. Other bands of humans domesticated the animals they once followed, learned to use the milk they supplied and, being reluctant to kill their food source, adopted largely vegetarian diets.

Whatever pattern of life was chosen, the survivors were those humans who were best adapted to following the life pattern of the group. So the people who left the river bank by the land route became differentiated according to how an economic relationship was built up around the fauna and the flora of the newly penetrated area. To facilitate this differentiation, humans evolved in terms of physical characteristics, giving rise to ethnic differences that reflected adaptations to particular terrains. So Evolution generated particular types of build: stockily built people who could run fast and were well adapted to the chase; tall people who could spot predators lying in wait for the cattle; narrow-eyed people who gained some protection from the blinding effects of desert storms; hairy people, insulated against the cold by flowing beards and moustaches to cover those parts of their unclothed bodies and who could cope with the privations of the Ice Age. Migrating people also developed skin colour adapted to the demands of particular environments. Dark skins offered protection against intense ultra-violet penetration by sunlight while light skins allowed for the greater utilization of vitamin D in sunlight in regions where long periods of darkness prevailed for much of the year. But in addition to those physical characteristics that could be observed, there were others that were internal and of which people would be unaware in social encounter. Immunity from diseases went with the denizens of particular territories. Tropical areas support a wide range of insects that carry disease or dangerous stings. The development of constitutional resistance would here play a key part in human survival. So as a consequence of the Great Migration humans became highly diversified. People chose the environment that best matched their physical characteristics while the environment in turn exerted its influence through natural selection on those physical features which offered a special advantage.

In this exodus from the river banks those who took the land route chose the most direct means of dispersing the human population as they fanned out over the land, so quickly relieving population density. These may be termed the *land-people*. The alternative mode of human dispersion was by water. For river dwellers the simple response to over-population was to take to floating logs or dug-out boats and to move downstream. That journey would eventually lead to a maritime area where ample supplies of sea-fish and molluscs offered a new rich source of diet. The coastal zone lends itself to a very simple form of harvesting and gathering. Each tide brings in its fresh crop of produce. Fish are easily trapped in shallow pools. Crustaceans which bury themselves in the sands can as readily be dug out again by those who know where to look. The coast offered a sure and regular harvest. Those who decided to regularize their life in this style were the *coastal-people*. This distinct group declined to move inland and never developed the sea-going boats that would enable them to harvest the full fruits of the sea. Such a specialized form of life could not be assured forever. Eventually they were destined to confront those who arrived at the coast by taking the longer land route. Yet in the primaeval era of *Homo sapiens* confrontation did not present an insuperable problem. Avoidance offered the perennial solution and the *coastal-people* merely moved further along the coast whenever they were free to do so. Coastal areas offer a greater continuity in what they can supply, unlike inland areas which vary greatly in their flora and fauna. The *coastal-people* travelled considerable distances and over the centuries were able to do so with only minimal changes in their life-style. Because the challenges and opportunities they faced were relatively constant, they were barely touched by the forces of natural selection. Hence the *coastal-people* remained among the most primitive of those who left the original habitat of *Homo sapiens*. Their former existence can be traced in isolated parts of the world through the relics of coastal habitations marked by the remains of shellfish. The last of these people, the aboriginal inhabitants of Tasmania, were in the unusual position of being an island people without boats. Eventually being unable to withstand competition from other populations who crowded in on them, the *coastal-people* were the first to become extinct.

Yet there were others who took the river route to the coast for whom brighter prospects lay ahead. Wider opportunities opened up for those discovering that greater potential wealth lay in the sea itself rather than in the coast. The sea contained larger fish and in ample supply. The challenge lay in adapting river craft so that they could become sea-worthy even if they did not venture far over the main. Once that challenge had been recognized and overcome, the ratio of effort versus results operated in their favour. In other words, the *fisher-folk* would expend less labour than *coastal-people* in meeting their necessary food requirements and so could use their greater leisure time for other purposes.

Yet there were even greater opportunities ahead for those who met the full challenge of the oceans. The lure of offshore islands offered prospects for monopolistic economic exploitation unavailable to either the *coastal-people* or the *land-people* as well as personal security and freedom from invaders and competitors. Those who welcomed this scenario were the *sea-people*, who eventually became a real force by exhibiting their mastery of the high seas. But first they had to overcome a series of formidable challenges. The first was to design craft that could withstand storms at sea and offer a reasonable degree of safety. Secondly, their vessels needed to become larger than fishing-boats, since their cargoes would include both people and goods. That in turn meant that more investment was needed in terms of materials and manufacturing time. It would take many hours of labour to construct a reliable sea-going vessel, while a shortage of suitable materials would act as a further limitation.

THE FOUR MAIN MIGRATORY GROUPS IN ORDER OF THE CHALLENGES THEY FACED

THE SEA-PEOPLE

Sea-worthy ships
Precision navigation
Storage of food and
drink for long
sea voyages

THE LAND-PEOPLE

Unfamiliar terrain
Migrating fast-moving
animals
Drought

THE FISHER-FOLK

Construction of nets
Unpredictability of
fish stocks

THE COASTAL-PEOPLE

The limitations of
beach combing
The need to keep moving

In terms of group-size, the *land-people* had the benefit of occupying larger areas of territory than the *coastal-people*, the *fisher-folk* or the *sea-people*. Their great hinterland could support a larger population. In any struggle for territory in primaeval society the larger groups had the upper hand and the others merely moved away. Those with the advantage of boats were well placed to cross the mouth of estuaries or sail to off-shore islands and so to distance themselves from the enveloping *land-people*.

While *sea-people* proved the most immune to the incursions of the *land-people*, for they could put more water between them and the invaders, distance comes at a price. Long-distance travel demands that new technical challenges need to be overcome. Sea water might be ideal for bathing, but it does not make drinking water. Just as new developments were required in boat design, so also new water storage vessels were needed, adequate in size to meet the demands of sea voyages. Food storage also needed special consideration with the ever-present problem of salt-contamination or bacterial deterioration. Technology in one development usually prompts another and creates the conditions for the innovative society.

But one wider effect of changing technology is the change it renders on the interpretation of the natural world. A proactive approach to Nature displaces taboos with all their inhibitions. Cause and effect take precedence over magic spells. An outward looking society has its eyes on the far horizons. That is the situation that prevailed when primaeval men became seafarers and looked out to that distant world where the sky meets the sea. For men the challenge was there. Exploration is genetically built into the psyche of the male, for the distant domain is one that belongs to *him*. But for women it was another matter. The remote domain was not part of *their* domain. For them it was a *foreign* domain that would be hedged around with taboos against female entry. Men who entered it must have appeared at great risk, which is why so much sympathetic magic was practised to ensure their safe return. Since time immemorial ships have been lost at sea and even today modern fishing trawlers are lost with all hands. When primaeval men first became seafarers, the losses must have been immense. Yet those losses produced long-term gains. They enabled a step forward to be taken in human progress both on the biological front and in the acquisition of knowledge.

The Grim Reaper would certainly have exercised his merciless hand in natural selection, so that many sailors and fishermen sank beneath the waves. But those who survived differed from those who perished. The survivors were proven masters in knowledge of the elements; they had learned something about cause and effect; they learned about the properties of materials and of their reaction to sea water; they could apply knowledge and understanding to the design of the ships on which they sailed. Those who perished had preponderantly failed to *take the lessons on board* (a phrase that has now acquired a broader meaning in the English language). The ultimate benefit to follow from losses at sea came as a gain in corporate memory. Even when great seamen ultimately died, their learning would pass on to the next generation through tradition and so could be reactivated for future use. Natural selection operated through thousands of years to produce a superbreed of sailors and of ships even before the cities of civilization came into existence.

But one thing was missing from the ships of the early prehistoric era: women. Long established custom meant that they would stay at home in their tribal villages praying for the safe return of the men. They would greet returning heroes and

'If you think we're coming on board that on the next voyage, you're mistaken.'

welcome the booty they had gleaned from the deep and from far distant shores. But to climb on board and agree to set sail to promising lands was quite a different matter. That hesitation would not be easily overcome. Women had consolidated their crucial role in primaeval society by adhering to their position as contractors with men as their suppliers. If ships were to become their home in oceanic voyages, so being incorporated into the female domain, women demanded ships that would meet their specification in the functions of seaworthiness and amenities. The needs of small children were paramount, for they could not be left behind. Primaeval women were not easily satisfied. They wanted proof or at least convincing evidence that the journey would be safe, that they would arrive at their destination and that such a sea voyage would be worthwhile.

These demands renewed among men the pursuit of excellence in terms of the design of ships and navigation. Little direct evidence survives about how these ships were constructed, for being made of biodegradable material they could not outlast the erosion of great stretches of time. We only know that vast distances were travelled, since remote islands were populated in prehistoric times and there are archaeological pointers to trans-oceanic travel.

It is clear that the *sea-people* knew a great deal about navigation and that they used the stars as guidelines. They could locate small islands in vast oceans taking into account the long-cycle movements of the stars. They understood the rotation of the planets within the solar system. Recent interpretations of the arrangement of marker stones and prehistoric monuments in very different parts of the world bear out the remarkable understanding of stellar constellations by prehistoric humans. The setting out of monoliths to serve as calendars revealed also an extraordinary understanding of mathematics, a capacity that was further demonstrated in the precision with which buildings were constructed during the Stone Age. Science and mathematics became established subjects during the era of prehistoric man. All that knowledge can stem from oceanic travel, sifted and tested in practice over a great span in time. How then is such intellectual prowess to be reconciled with those primitive modes of thinking that are so widespread in aboriginal societies and are presumed to have been prevalent in primaeval communities of that Age?

The explanation I will offer is a corrective to the view that humans are intrinsically intelligent. I will reiterate instead my earlier point that *Homo sapiens* is no more intelligent than our predecessors and former contemporaries – Neanderthal man. The human mind operates by association thinking, which gives us sympathetic and contagious magic. *Intelligent thought* is a social product arising through communication in pursuit of an objective where the notions developed are cast in a setting where their exploration can be tested in practice. Ideas that are formulated and put to the test also need to be discussed. A small team, comprising individuals who can make complementary contributions, maximizes effective communication between its members. Beyond a certain size the members of a group cannot communicate effectively and productively with one another. They are then obliged to communicate through a leader. This simplifies the business of communication but distorts its natural dynamism. The leader will impose his own thoughts and others act as respondents, being usually reluctant to challenge the leader. Teams and groups may both have objectives but, as a team is smaller than a group, each team member has the greater opportunity to learn through interpersonal discussion. In the case of the larger group, the objective may be far removed from each member's relevant experience or interests. So individuals will learn little from one another. Their frame of reference is limited by the demand placed upon them by the group leader. Small teams united in purpose and learning together act intelligently and develop a mode of thinking which creates its own momentum.

When the *sea-people* embarked on long voyages in their proven sea vessels, taking their women-folk with them, they needed to be sure where they were going. To master that art they had become astronomers. Astronomy developed as people used the stars for a purpose. But eventually for those whose fortunes and security did not depend on the stars, as was the case with the *land-people*, other uses were seen for these shining signposts of the firmament. The stars were controllers of people. The stars controlled human destinies. The stars were the homes of the gods. But the *sea-people* thought in different terms. They could dispense with the luxury of mythology, for they were bound by the perils of the sea and the overriding need to focus on pragmatism. The master mariners of ancient times had always operated in that size of human unit that has proved the most durable and most effective – the small team.

The reason was compelling enough. Only a small number of people could build and board a sea-faring vessel. There was no surplus space for others. The absence of passenger liners in the prehistoric era gave the *sea-people* a special and privileged position. But as the once empty spaces of continents filled with rising populations of *land-people*, the *sea-people* eventually found themselves in the minority whenever there were population encounters, for natural selection had taken its toll. The *sea-people*, coming from small communities anyway, had suffered relatively large population losses on the oceans in the course of mastering those skills that made them pre-eminent voyagers. Their numbers meant that they could not afford military engagements with the more populous *land-people*. They looked for islands that could offer private occupation. Wherever they went they endeavoured to erect marker-stones or conspicuous religious buildings that would signal to others that they were in possession and would ward off prospective colonists.

What was remarkable about the *sea-people* was that their quest for privacy and security was counter-balanced by an outgoing attitude towards other peoples. The *sea-people*, unlike their

'It looks as though this place is already occupied.'

47

brethren the *fisher-folk*, had developed an economy that depended on the making of contacts. As entrepreneurs of the seas they would trade, wherever they could, with other sea-board communities, introducing new products or acting as carriers. They needed to be welcomed and reciprocally they welcomed others to their island sanctuaries. Indeed, the conditions they offered in terms of civilized living made them net beneficiaries of a *brain-drain* from surrounding areas. That in turn increased their capacity to offer an increasing range of professional skills to the *land-people*. But they could always retreat, when danger threatened, to the safety of the islands whence they came. The proviso was that the *land-people* could not get across.

The *sea-people* maintained their superiority on the oceans for a long period during which they became a repository for the mathematical and scientific knowledge of the era. Their influence was felt for centuries in agriculture and building construction as their skills were passed on from one people to another. But the seafaring and ship-building skills were also transmitted in due course and in a similar fashion. With that loss of monopoly the golden age of the *sea-people* was coming to an end. Now in the aftermath of the Great Migration, Power shifted in the direction of larger forces. The *land-people* began to wield an increasing influence on world events due to their greater numbers. Yet denser populations created unfamiliar organizational scenarios, for which previous solutions were no longer an option. With the response to that challenge, a new form of human evolution was to be set in motion.

In retrospect, the Age of Migration rewarded the adventurous. The first people to reach virgin territory could claim the land for themselves and, for a while, reap its fruits unhindered by other challengers. Yet exploring is not synonymous with hunting. Hunter–gatherers do not necessarily explore, for they often confine themselves to a known terrain. Exploration needs a bold outlook, skill and adaptability and can ultimately lead to better hunting, if the challenges can be overcome, for game is usually difficult to locate and will usually seek seclusion as a means of self-preservation. Exploring potentially adds to resources – the discovery of fresh water, promising camping sites, fertile soils and useful caves that can provide shelter and storage for food. Large-scale migration followed in the wake of exploration, resulting in the dispersion of the human species and the emergence of new human characteristics. Each population eventually made its own distinctive adjustment to the habitat on which it settled. The resulting ethnic diversity produced a widening range of human attributes, eventually setting the scene for an accelerating pace in human evolution. Natural selection now began to exert its relentless pressure on the new arrivals in territories that were no longer virgin but disputed. A new era was opening, leaving behind an age of relative tranquillity in contrast to the new age that was to follow.

PART TWO

THE AGE OF POWER

Preview

Once the most habitable lands had become occupied, Evolution found a new form of competitive advantage. Rather than focusing on developing a stable relationship within an existing territory, more was to be gained by removing others from their territories. This challenge demanded a new breed of humans. And so it came about that large groups controlled by powerful leaders would overrun small communities. The conquered were either wiped out or enslaved. Women, who had played vital roles in primaeval society, were reduced to subservience and deprived of their original economic and political functions. Conquerors used Terror to reach their goals and Terror to maintain their position as Rulers. Yet, economically, their absolute power brought certain advantages, for it facilitated the creation of new divisions of labour. Useful captives were spared, set up in ghettos and protected. And so, as the Age of Power reached its zenith, natural selection favoured the survival of three different segments of the population – the aggressive and victorious, the usefully talented and the generally subservient. But Terror ultimately became counter-productive as violence and cruelty stoked up rebellion. People began to lose confidence in their Rulers and turned to religion in which Righteousness replaced

Power. Alerted to the dangers, Rulers recovered by supporting a religion based on an Almighty whose demands on the masses reflected those of the Ruler. Yet it was not enough. Power continued to lose its grip as a result of the increasing technical advances emanating from the division of labour. With the invention of printing, education spread. Women found a new route towards emancipation. At the same time new vigorous communities, separated by seas and mountains beyond the reach of Rulers, began to exert an increasing influence and presence. Rulers found it increasingly difficult to maintain their absolute grip. Just as internal forces were undermining the credibility of absolute Power, so also external forces were impinging on the boundaries of Empire.

4

The fall of Eve

With the exception of stone tools and stone blocks used in buildings, the oldest artefacts manufactured by humans are female figurines. These figurines survive in small numbers yet have been found in widely separated parts of the world. The most notable examples are well rounded with pendulous breasts, large stomachs and buttocks and project the essence of physical femininity. More rarely other figurines are found, skinny or evidently pregnant or menstruating, since traces of red ochre occur near their genitalia. In general, most of these figurines have little or no head. But occasionally one is discovered with an evident hair-style. So what overall meaning can be attached to these relics of the remotest past?

There has been much speculation: they were goddesses; they were fertility symbols facilitating the growth of crops; they were sexual reminders of home for those embarked on a long-distance hunt. Whatever their origin, these figurines offer testimony to the esteem with which women were held in primaeval communities. Women were the givers of life. More-over, they are now reckoned to have played a major role in the economic life of hunter–gatherers, and more so in earlier than later periods. The reason is simple. Men did not make very good hunters. They ran after their prey but their prey could run faster. They used throwing sticks to injure animals, which would then be pursued and killed once they had caught up with them. But it took a lot of running. Men needed to be good long distance runners and it is significant perhaps that the greatest concentration of world class marathon runners exists today in a tribe inhabiting the very valley in Kenya where the oldest specimens of *Homo sapiens* have been unearthed. It is not unusual for predators to have low rates of success in catching their prey. There is mutual self-interest for each species in some degree of failure. Only if success rates are low can the prey continue to survive on their given territory and so offer opportunities for later generations of predators. Where the success rates for early hunters were low, they were obliged to rely on scavenging – getting to the kills of other predators and driving them off.

When the hunting is not so good the well-being of the human community depends on gathering, that role which had become a female speciality. Knowing which fruits and plants to collect and which are poisonous and how to make best use of the overall produce provide the basis for an assured existence and even a welcome cuisine. Women in the earliest times could guarantee food in a way that men could not. But the balance began to change as tools improved. Throwing-sticks were replaced by wooden spears, wooden spears by shafts tipped with flints and, in turn, tipped spears by arrow heads. The trapping of fish in pools gave way to netting them in streams and lakes. The development of digging tools for the extraction of flints led to the digging of covered pits into which the lured larger prey fell, were entrapped and easily despatched. In time the ability of men to improve their efficiency in contributing to the food supply of the community raised their status within it relative to that of women. This change in the balance of society affected a number of social practices but was less than fundamental. In terms of natural selection, the greater male contribution towards the economy did nothing to change the genetic disposition of men and women towards the activities they undertook.

The position of women in the primaeval communities of the original homelands had owed much to the extent of the female domain, which in effect corresponded with the immediate area of human habitation. The role of men centred on the domain that lay beyond, which acted as a supply and resource reservoir. As men mainly met women within the boundaries of the female domain, the influence of women over men had been considerable. But during the period of the migration, the relationship of the two genders was affected. Women would inevitably spend more time than usual outside their own domain and therefore came to a greater extent under male influence. Settlement in new locations provided the opportunity for women to restore the balance in their relationship. But that was now more difficult to re-establish given prolonged exposure to the male domain, where hunting and exploration figured prominently.

At the end of the Great Migration, when the inhabitable areas of the world had been fully explored, further factors propelled cultures away from restoration of the female domain. Male domination grew as violence figured increasingly on the agenda. The most favoured territories for settlement now needed to be fought for and, if secured, to be vigorously defended. Over-population could no longer be easily solved by colonization, for few new communities could be established without trespassing on occupied territory. There was always an element of uncertainty as to which people occupied which land, there was no means of agreeing where the frontier lay, and in the case of communities that followed seasonal migrating patterns, acknowledged frontiers did not exist. The only way of establishing the territorial position was through constant probing. Two adjacent communities therefore developed a partly antagonistic and partly neighbourly relationship with one another. Genetically they still came from much the same stock so that ways of the primaeval community still exercised a strong pull on their behaviour. Being adjacent communities they were orientated towards exogamous marriages in keeping with past traditions. These would take place in the normal way until they became interrupted by skirmishes along disputed frontiers. The emotionally charged outfall then made it very difficult to bring about agreed inter-marriages. But the aim could be achieved by other means. As escalating skirmishes generated deaths and exacerbated relationships, skirmishes eventually turned into punitive raids. A raiding party would attack a village, killing opponents in a pre-emptive strike against a perceived threat. In so doing, force would perpetuate the practice of exogamous marriages, allowing the successful raiding party to make off with young women for wives in a practice known as *wife-stealing*.

Wife-stealing was not, however, a fully effective substitute for exogamous marriages. As relationships were not reciprocal but one-sided, the raided village was less well placed to collect wives in the same way. Still, potential wives on both sides of the border remained attracted to exogamous marriages for reasons that may have been unconscious but which served a real function in terms of the positive effect on the genetic stock. While there were pressures therefore to resume practices normal for primaeval communities, these practices had to be modified rather than restarted in their original form. The solution came in the form of *ritualized wife-stealing*. A mock raid would be made on a village. There would be ritualized opposition and the raiders would make off with a wife. The raided village would then make a return ritualized raid on the village of the raiders and another wife would be whisked away in the face of mock opposition. From a genetic point of view such practices offered a satisfactory precaution against the ills of in-breeding. Wife-stealing also helped to solve an internal social problem. The true primaeval community was basically monogamous. Men were socially bonded together in their hunting groups. For one man in the party to have cuckolded another in the event of a scarcity of wives would have destroyed the co-operative nature of their joint activities and jeopardized the economy. Infidelity was more than an interpersonal issue. As a violation of accepted taboos it posed risks for the whole community. It was not that primaeval people were prudish, for given the higher mortality rate of men, widows would be passed on as second wives, often to brothers of the deceased. Tribal tradition played a very important part in the Age of Respect. Women were treated as desirable rather than as generally available and exploitable sexual objects.

However, in the new era that was developing repeated disputes over territory gave rise to some groups becoming more successful than others. Wife-stealing, instead of being preceded by a mock battle, now entailed real fighting. The differing strengths of the combatants meant that wife-stealing became a one-way traffic rather than a reciprocal arrangement. Since the basic objective of the raid was to kill those offending and responsible for skirmishes, the women taken in a surprise raid increasingly became unwilling victims. While the aim of a raid would not be to exterminate the enemy, but only to take punitive and preventative action, captured women would be treated as a reward for a successful mission and be brought back to base. But the price of that victory was to violate the previously understood customs that had long prevailed in the primaeval community based on reciprocal exogamy. The acquisition of wives, surplus to needs, changed the dominant position of primaeval woman in her own domain. She now had domestic intruders forced upon her and operating in the role of sexual competitors.

The aftermath of raids that grew in intensity fostered conflict between men and women for it brought into question their respective roles. Did women retain their control over the local domain? Or should captured women be treated as belonging to the same broad categories as weapons (and the trophies they offer) in which case they fell into the male domain? That conflict in possession of the domain was intensified when in the fullness of time wars replaced raids. Such a consequence was almost inevitable. Skirmishes generate feuds that can grow in magnitude and seldom disappear entirely. Wars offer a certain attraction by removing the problem once and for all. By killing all male opponents the lands of the defeated can be taken over and occupied by the victor's surplus population.

Large-scale territorial victories, however, bring in their wake a new population problem. Women are predominantly non-combatants in wars. If the men are slaughtered, what happens to the women? Unless the women are massacred along with their menfolk, they have to be taken in and found a role. This was no longer a simple matter comparable in nature with the consequence of a raid, where captured women could serve merely to 'top up' the existing female population in the community. Where war leads to the capture of the *entire* female population of the enemy, a more radical solution is needed.

One possibility was to treat the captives as auxiliary wives, which would violate established tribal practice. Primaeval women would resist erosion of their traditional rights. Another was to treat captured women as slaves, so potentially minimizing objections from wives by offering 'help in the house'. These types of issue were usually settled in primaeval society by consensus. But in the last resort the issue could be settled by Power. When consensus gives way to Power, women lose all influence, for once gender conflict arises women are no match for men.

The social consequences of territorial conflict and expansion were that women lost effective control over what had formerly been their domain and over which male dominion increasingly extended. Women were forced to give up claims to that domain over which they had been genetically equipped to exercise their rights throughout a very long evolutionary period. As polygamy sprang from the fruits of conquest the best compromise was to persuade their husbands to house additional wives in separate huts and to maintain as far as possible some limited authority in the household and the community.

Conquest brought in its wake a further problem. The gender-related division of labour, along with the co-ordinating function of continuing sexual intimacy, had become the cornerstone for community regulation. Once women began to lose their key role, that formula no longer applied. The focus of attention moved from the domestic and local scene to the winning of battles. Successful operations in warfare gain from the deployment of larger numbers than the enemy can muster. A large fighting force requires a new division of labour with specialized weaponry and tactics and a hierarchy to regulate effort and formulate strategy. That switch in emphasis was to have a radical effect on female participation in the affairs of the community, diminishing their role and maximizing the role of men. The only sure way of bringing about this transfer was through forceful imposition. So the archetypal gender-related division of labour was displaced by a revised approach. It first made its mark in the military field, and was then extended to cover the whole social scene.

The position of women as active role-players in society was further affected as a consequence of the prolonged absence of men, which happened as wars replaced raids or skirmishes. Wars take longer to finish. The problem then arises that women left behind during the duration of the war might be enticed to engage in liaisons with other men. The taboos of the primaeval community might once have precluded adultery. But under these new conditions taboos began to lose their cogency as a form of social self-regulation. Fighting men were now firmly in control on the domestic front and being away at the wars for much of the time they demanded a guarantee of fidelity from wives. In medieval Europe the solution was the chastity belt. Yet as a solution its applications were regionally restricted since it required a certain degree of engineering knowledge. In different parts of the world other solutions were found, these being what are technically known as cliteridectomy, infibulation and claustration.

First consider the practice of cliteridectomy. In Chapter 1 attention was drawn to the importance of specialized sexual anatomy in facilitating the continued liaison of men and women and the central role of the clitoris in activating continuing female interest in men. This organ was now considered a solution to the fidelity problem. The clitoris could be cut out at puberty in a painful operation leaving women less interested in sex and therefore less tempted by infidelity in the absence of the male warrior. In the Age of Power, as women lost their position in

'Just off for four years. Meanwhile no locksmith is permitted entry to the castle.'

influencing men, brutality invaded the domestic domain. Female circumcision was demanded before marriage took place and eventually became ritualized. A second, even more brutal refinement, guaranteeing security against infidelity, was infibulation. The labia of the vagina were sewn up to prevent entry of the male organ while still allowing the passing of water. That practice still continues today but appears to be dying out. Certainly it is not as commonly practised as female circumcision, which is well established in a number of regions of the world in spite of the efforts of the World Health Organisation to eradicate the custom.

It is easy to comprehend the purpose of female circumcision and easier still the practice of infibulation, but what about male circumcision (the excision of the foreskin of the penis)? What is the purpose of its removal? Its original existence can scarcely be functionless in the context of primaeval society. That function is evidently to protect the prepuce of the penis and to retain its sensitivity to the corresponding part of the female genitalia. Its possible physical contribution to the success of the primaeval community lies in aiding sexual bonding. Male circumcision is more widespread today than female circumcision and takes place immediately after birth, when the innocent child is powerless to protest, or at puberty where the practice marks the initiation of youth into manhood. Why then should the foreskin be removed in a painful operation that detracts from its original anatomical function?

To answer that question one has only to look at those periods of history where it was *imposed*. They belong to the age of conquest and genocide. The rape and seizure of women became part of the booty that conquering soldiers were promised. Without that incentive mercenary soldiers, for example, were reluctant to leave their homes for long military campaigns. So slaves, captured in battle and enrolled as *janisseries* in the service of the Ottoman Empire, were obligatorily circumcised before they were armed as soldiers. The reason was simple enough and it has to do with hygiene. Free sexual access to women increases the chance of sexual infections and so lowers the effectiveness of the army. Bacteria can be stored and carried beneath the foreskin. Circumcision offers a degree of protection. Condoms offer far more effective protection at the present day, but still male circumcision continues. The origins of circumcision, however, reach far back in time but their origins are most conspicuous in areas that have been heavily fought over.

One can therefore return to the question of whether female and male circumcision are related. The answer appears to be in the affirmative. In the case of female circumcision the objective is to *restrict* sexual opportunity; in the case of men the objective is to *increase* it. If conquered women are to be sexually exploited, men have to be sexually protected. On the other hand men need the guarantee that their own wives will not engage in sexual adventures with other men.

Whatever the suffering of women resulting from genital mutilation, such practices, it might be argued, operated in the interest of evolution. The absence of men at war might reduce the reproduction rate in the short term. But by striving to expand the territory available to the particular strains of the human species, these fighting men were serving the greater interest of the species-strain rather than merely themselves as individuals. Those strains of humans who win new territory expand their population, while those who lose theirs perish.

Finally one comes to the practice of claustration (the shutting up of women). While sexual mutilation of women might act as a safeguard against women *voluntarily* eloping with other men, the practice offers no protection against *involuntary* seizure. In the Age of Power nothing left unguarded was safe. When men were away at war women were at risk of being grabbed by raiders, especially by slave-traders. So, along the traditional slave routes, women became subject to a new restriction, being in effect incarcerated at home or forbidden to enter into public activity, except in certain circumstances where they were enveloped by clothing that neutralized their female shapes. In so far as they were excluded from economic activities involving social mixing, the male domain grew further at their expense. The more dangerous a region the greater the curtailment placed on the movement of women. Hence in some parts of the world, as subsistence economies gave way to simple market economies, women were kept from market. Thereby they were restricted from engaging in those very activities of 'gathering and communicating' which was basic to their nature in primaeval society.

All these extreme measures against women were undertaken without regard to their interests and must have been vigorously resented and resisted. That resistance in turn produced a male backlash. Whereas in the primaeval community women were worshipped as the givers of life and respected for their magical powers, they were now seen as potentially undermining the stability and virility of society. The old myths of creation with their distinctly individual stories, characterizing each tribal group, now gave way to a more general story of creation in which the source of troubles could be laid at the door of women. It was Eve who ate the forbidden apple and brought all the troubles on the World; it was Pandora who opened the box and allowed all the sins to escape. Women were used as the totem of Disobedience, a clear sign that its converse state, Obedience, had become the new value in the Age of Power. The folly and sin of Disobedience, so conspicuously represented in legend and so conspicuously associated with women, testifies to the resistance they offered to the invasion of their domain. But that resistance was all in vain. As the world became divided into territories over which tribes fought to maintain or improve their share, and as prehistory moved into history, the role of women diminished to the extent that they lost effective control of their relationships. Marriages were arranged by men without consultation solely in the interests of male ambition in respect of riches, property and territory. In losing control over anything that could be recognized as their traditional domain, women became totally subject to rule by men.

The way in which the loss of woman's role was engineered throughout the Age of Power raises the matter of how far it has produced permanent effects. War and conquest accelerate genetic changes by exercising a form of 'natural selection'. Killing has been selective and has impinged differently on men and women. Males from defeated populations have been spared for their *occupational usefulness*. The best craftsmen and professionals, whose skills were reckoned economically indispensable for the successful city or nation, were spared, relocated in ghettos and afforded every protection. In contrast, I find no historical evidence that women have been treated in a similar way. The basis of their selection for survival has been an assessment of how far they could contribute to the leisure needs of men. The estimated assets of captured women revolved round their ability to entertain through the arts of dance, music, singing, poetry and above all, erotic activity. If the skills of men and women are gender-related, the Age of Power maximized the differences. It brought about the situation where the *belief* that men were more able and clever became self-fulfilling. If excellent selected craftsmen are introduced into the city, then the need for an extension of skills points in the direction of men, with their proven capacities, rather than in the direction of women.

A belief in the different qualities of men and women was endorsed by the earliest female philosophers, whose writings in an era about 2,400 years ago survive only as fragments. These moral philosophers from the Greek Aegean world, including Aesara, Phintys and Perictione, wrote eloquently about balance and harmony and its application to law and justice. Phintys in particular addressed herself to the differences between men and women. She wrote:

> *I think some things are peculiar to a man, some to a woman, some are common to both, some belong more to a man than a woman, some more to a woman than a man. Peculiar to a man are serving in battle, political activity, and public speaking; peculiar to a woman are staying at home and indoors, and welcoming and serving her husband . . . Excellences of the body are health, strength, keenness of perception and beauty. Some of these are more fitting for a man to cultivate and possess, some more to a woman. For courage and* **wisdom** *are more appropriate for a man, both because of the constitution of his body and because of the strength of his soul, while moderation is more appropriate for a woman.* (From *A History of Women Philosophers*, vol. 1: *600 b.c. – 500 a.d.*, Kluwer Academic Publishers, Dordrecht, 1987, ed. M.A. Waite.)

Even at this early stage in recorded history when women were still significant members of society in their own right, it is evident that the status of women had already declined to some degree. Wisdom was now a male virtue where once it had been a quality of women. Wisdom itself was associated with the goddess Athene, the emblem of Athens. Wisdom has been attributed to women among some of the earliest peoples about whom palaeoanthropology has unearthed information. In line with this gender dichotomy the male gods of Athens had less reputable characters, being prone to drinking, womanizing and deception.

To trace the transition from female gods to male gods and finally to a single male god, the Almighty, is rendered difficult by the extent of the time-span. The latter period is covered by recorded history but the earlier stage in the train of events is shrouded in pre-history. That is where one is obliged to rely on legend. In the case of Athene, legend has it that the people of Athens voted in the market place on a god who would become the emblem of the city. In those days both men and women were entitled to vote. The women proposed Athene, while the men nominated Poseidon, the god of the sea. In the resulting ballot Athene emerged the winner. Later, women lost the right to vote. But in spite of this reverse for women, the city retained the goddess Athene as its emblem. If this legend reflects reality, the supposed origins of democracy now seem dubious. Hitherto, it was believed that democratic balloting was the product of a highly sophisticated society whose roots go back to Athens at the height of the classical period. Now we are compelled to entertain an alternative proposition: that democracy originated in a much earlier period and that much of its character was lost as civilization grew. Civilization brought in slavery and democracy gave ground to oligarchy. This earlier period was operationally closer to primaeval society. In other words, the roots of democracy lie in primaeval society, being characterized by the existence and importance of consensus. The difference between democracy and consensus is that the former involves a greater sophistication in method. However, as consensus became more difficult to bring about in more populous communities, the character of democracy changed and was weakened.

The Age of Power widened the differences between men and women, changed the esteem in which women were held and diversified the range of economic activities available to society as a whole, channelling them in the direction of men. So the division of labour instead of pivoting around the differences between men and women, as in primaeval society, now increasingly switched to divisions between sub-groups of men. The general boosting of the division of labour accelerated the sophistication of society. Evolution thereby found a formula for advancing the biological competitiveness of *Homo sapiens* and increasing its domination over Mother Earth. Yet such progress was made at a price. The gender balance that existed in primaeval society, and on which the earliest women philosophers placed such store, was largely lost. Men became entirely dominant in what now became a patriarchal society.

Could one conclude from such a trend that the male gender had evolved by natural selection to become better fitted to match the occupational needs of a society now cast in a hierarchical mould? And would the Age of Power leave its genetic mark on the succeeding Age, so posing new problems for gender relationships? These are questions that I will revisit in Chapters 9, 10 and 11. Meanwhile the story of human evolution continues.

Chapter
5

Advance of the Conqueror

Whenever population growth depends on the retention and expansion of territory, aggression and effectiveness in mobilizing resources to beat rivals become the dominating factors in natural selection. Inevitably for such a struggle some strains of humans were better suited than others. The most favourably placed were the hunters. Hunters had developed weapons specially adapted for killing large game. Such weapons could equally well be turned against rival humans in the contest for territory. Hunters were also socially ready. Since hunters cannot run as fast as their quarry, they need to resort to co-operative action in developing tactics and preparing ambushes. Their ability to operate as an emotionally bonded team meant that only minor modifications of their natural behaviour were needed for military engagements. Hunters also had the nutritional advantages of consuming meat. Their protein-rich diet provided a long-lasting supply of energy, leaving them ample time in which to improve their tools and discuss their strategies. Being accustomed to leaving home to track down large animals, offering the greatest prizes, they were ready to endure a long and demanding campaign of war.

When it came to martial struggle some strains of humans, though well endowed with skills and talents, were scarcely in a position to battle with the hunters. Foremost among these were the sea-people, whose protein came largely from fish but who could supplement their economies through trading across waters. Their ability to navigate had given them sophisticated knowledge of astronomy and had led on to calculations that could serve a wider set of purposes, including the building of defensive fortifications and the sowing of crops according to the seasons. Yet those skills were not enough to enable them to compete on equal terms with hunters. In the ultimate analysis those who live by what they can catch from the sea lack the ready-made weapons to face better-equipped enemies. Fishing nets are no match for hunting weapons, a point made evident in show matches with gladiators in Roman arenas at a later date when the Age of Power was at its zenith. That apart, the sea-people could not afford the human losses that war brings, for their limitations lay in their relatively small numbers. Ships in ancient times could not support a population of a size comparable with what was possible in boundless land settlements. Yet for this threatened population as a whole there was always a way out. The sea-people could escape in their ships, so avoiding military engagements on unfavourable terms. Being better placed than other groups to find safe havens, they could find

'Stop making and growing and do something useful. There's a city waiting to be raided over there.'

sanctuary on islands, where they could carry on their way of life undisturbed.

For other strains of humans it was less easy to find a permanent solution to the invasion of their territories by the hunters. The pastoralists and herders, whose wealth lay in their cattle and who supplemented their diets with crops, had no adequate defences, possessing neither the weapons of the hunters nor the skills of the sea-people. As traditional migrants, they therefore opted for avoidance, giving up disputed territory and searching for other areas in which they could survive without harassment.

Natural selection began to operate in its relentless way on these various strains of humans with their distinctive characteristics and life-styles who did not move out of the path of the would-be conquerors. The consequence of the struggle was that populations based on hunting expanded at the expense of other groups. So aggression replaced co-operation as the primary factor in determining population growth. The winners took over the territories best fitted for human habitation, pushing out the existing population into less hospitable terrain or killing them if they failed to flee. Yet some of the losers in the struggle for territory were assimilated by the winning group and so contributed to both the genetic and cultural inheritance of the victors. The mathematical and astronomical skills of the sea-people were brought in to provide solutions to a range of problems that varied from navigation for purposes of trade, to the design of large buildings as cities became the basis of urban civilization. The permanent nature of these cities took shape as buildings were constructed of durable materials like stone in place of degradable materials such as wood. Crops were now sown in a planned rotation that fitted with an astronomical reading of the seasons. Subject groups of land-people made their influence felt by incorporating the metal technologies used in the development of their hunting weapons and now diverted into instruments of war. Other groups of land-people contributed their knowledge of cattle management and the technologies that sprang from the use of leather.

The former hunters therefore enriched their material and cultural life and were no longer obliged to live by the chase. They benefited from the enlargement of their genetic contribution to the surviving human stock and from the cultural gains. But at heart they were still hunters. Aggression had secured the territory on which their stock could be increased. Now, as populations continued to expand, a new form of contest began. The organized hunters were no longer pitted against weaker opponents but against their own kind as less competitive breeds and societies were pushed aside. Small wars continued in a form of warring stalemate that for thousands of years did little to change the direction and make-up of the human stock. Raised aggression and well-developed hand weapons failed to tilt decisively the balance between the various tribal warring groups.

However, aggression *per se* could not ensure victory over disputed territories, for one overriding factor is numbers. In general, large groups overwhelm small groups. Personal aggressiveness and large numbers together form a winning combination. Even a small tribe by uniting with another can overwhelm a large neighbour, as Ghengis Khan discovered. Thereafter the formula was for one tribe to attack another, to create terror for those who resisted while offering a role to those who submitted. Those who yielded were allowed to become junior followers of the dominant group. The larger combined force was then strong enough to overwhelm more distant nations, to seize their territory and so create an empire. Size produces a decisive pay-off in military engagements. Just as in the animal kingdom, where the physical size of creatures gives them an evolutionary advantage over smaller creatures with the proviso that they do not outrun the available food supply, so also this human variation of the size formula played a dominant role in military history. In other words, large well-disciplined groups are most likely to triumph in battle.

Whenever victories arise in succession the invading force needs to put into immediate operation its policies towards the defeated. Those policies can only be inferred in relation to much of the pre-literate world. As it happened, the Israelites were among the earliest of the literate peoples and they set out in detail how those policies should operate in relation to their entry into the Promised Land (Deuteronomy 20: 10–18):

> *Of the cities of the Promised Land; namely, the Hittites and the Amorites, the Canaanites and the Perizzites, the Hivites and the Jebusites ... thou shall save nothing alive that breatheth....Of the cities far off: if it shall make peace ... then*

all the people found therein shall be tributaries unto thee, and
shall serve thee. . . . If it will not make peace with thee, then
thou shalt smite every male thereof with the edge of the sword:
but the women and the little ones and the cattle . . . shalt thou
take unto thyself.

Such policies appear to have been widespread during the advance of the Conqueror and laid the foundation for the next stage of the universal story. There is a saying: 'what is won by the sword must be retained by the sword'. Victory opens up a large gap between victorious and defeated peoples. The defeated people have to be kept in a state of submission if Power is not to lose its grip. Armies need to be retained to guard against insurrection. The ultimate expression of Power was the institution of mass slavery. Slavery began with the deployment of captives. These were mainly women, favoured for being more submissive and, in the absence of their slaughtered menfolk, now available for sexual exploitation. After a further passage in time, changing conditions brought about a gender-shift in demand towards male slaves. Interest and a flourishing market in male slavery began as the group in Power undertook large-scale projects for which large amounts of manpower were required. For the erection of cities, temples, palaces, monuments and defensive works more labour was needed than local communities could supply.

The slaves themselves fell into categories within an ordered hierarchy. There were even important slaves, notably the *mame-lukes*, castrated as a safeguard against excessive ambition, and entrusted with high positions in the administration of empire. At the other end of the hierarchical scale there were those who suffered the greatest ill treatment. There were galley slaves, chained to their oars and whipped into greater efforts in rowing the larger vessels of the ancient world faster towards their destination; and there were the slaves who worked on the *latifundia* of Roman estates, famed for the mass crucifixion of those who once united in rebellion. Wars were started in order to secure a supply of slaves. Slaves became valued merchandise for which there was a ready international market. In relatively recent times a well-developed African slave trade was able to supply the manpower to create the cotton plantations of North America, the sugar plantations of Central America and the coffee plantations of South America.

This gross use of Power dehumanized society, destroying the system whereby all members of a community strive to know one another and to find common agreement through the intimacies of interpersonal communication. If unity of action demands consensus, that consensus would not be forthcoming in a divided society. Unity had to be imposed. Such imposition required the most dominant and aggressive male to become the unchallenged leader, a possibility facilitated by ousting or killing all rivals. Ruthless aggression had been bred into the male personality through a long period of evolution based on natural selection. With genetic aggression being at a premium in the winning of territory, it was inevitable that aggressive qualities would become accentuated in a warrior group.

The winning of territory and the capture of slaves allowed the victors to make more intensive use of the land available. Hitherto there had always been an optimum size for a human population on a territory. Division of labour is an essential requirement where denser populations need to be sustained on territories of any given size. Gender had produced the first division of labour in human society and continued to persist because it was biologically based. But now new divisions of labour had to be invented to meet more complex needs. These new divisions could be drawn up just as they had been in war when imposed by the leader. The most important of these developments lay in relation to the use of water, which would always play a key part in human living. The overwhelming need to support a larger population was to provide the communal labour needed to dig ditches and develop irrigation. Here the free and spontaneous behaviours that typified action in primaeval communities would not suffice to serve the central purpose. Communal action of a sophisticated nature needed a plan. That plan called for its implementation on the attention of the war leader, whose attention now had to turn to civic affairs. The more sophisticated the plan, the finer became the divisions of labour needed to bring it to fruition. Brawn needed its counterpart, brain. Effort would be fruitless without skill and craftmanship. The ruler and his minions would search for these aptitudes in short supply. Wherever they could be found, they were incorporated into the fold and rewarded. Craftsmen were separated out into sub-communities, within which they married, so providing new genetic strains of individuals with distinctive aptitudes and learning and so

71

offering a guarantee that their skills would be passed on from one generation to the next.

The social composition of these larger ruled societies depended on the furtherance of the distinction between dominance and submission. The old egalitarian basis of primaeval society went into terminal decline. In its place a new society emerged based on rulers and ruled set within an intricate pattern of hierarchical relationships. The dominant ruler would be supported by a small number of others who were given lesser ruling privileges and licensed on condition of submitting to the ruler himself. So submission combined with aggression became the new cocktail that constituted human society in the age of violence.

These historical events raise a number of general points. The general need for a dominant leader is greatest in the gatherings of large groups where the masses are inclined to fix their gaze on a single person. That would offer the occasion when the ruler's will was most immune to challenge while the behaviour of the attending masses would be at their most submissive. Yet large male gatherings generate aggressive behaviour based on the concentration of male pheromones and their effect on male behaviour. That behaviour needed to be harnessed or it needed to be deflected. It was harnessed whenever the Conqueror announced news of a great victory or the beginning of a new campaign. It was deflected when ritualized aggression characterized the institutional celebrations of large groups. Leading enemies or 'traitors' would be publicly executed in show celebrations and would serve as reminders of how Power was won.

But such occasions cannot remain forever features of the mass meeting. The successful Conqueror is bound to run out of defeated opponents. But within the empire there were always other victims who could be found and who could serve as reminders of where power lay. The solution was to turn the spilling of blood into a religious ceremony without destabilizing the existing order. Ceremonial human sacrifice was the answer. By being taken out of secular politics and being made the responsibility of a Chief Priest, human sacrifice would then act as spur to develop a doctrine in which Power was justified on religious grounds. The key to the success of that strategy lay in the alliance between the Chief Priest and the Conqueror.

Yet there was also another reason for cementing the alliance between the Chief Priest and the Conqueror. As the Conqueror set out to consolidate his position, the greater became the need to overcome all competing forms of allegiance. The most deeply rooted of these lay in the religious beliefs of primaeval people, the veneration of their ancestors and their perceived need to act in accordance with what was demanded by the souls and spirits they respected. Such a division in loyalty might operate to the detriment of the Conqueror's interests. The most feasible means of overcoming this potential source of trouble was the centralization of religion under the aegis of the priests. Now all competing forms of religion could be viewed as sacrilege and the supply of victims for sacrifice could be assured.

Religious ceremonies gave expression to the underlying values of the dominant group, which were projected in terms of blood and punishment, submission and humility. The cost to the Conqueror of devolving Power to a priestly class was some loss of control. The priests created a momentum of their own. Being reactive rather than proactive they had neither direct involvement nor interest in the economic activities of society. For them with their inward focus the stars now took on a magical significance. Rather than being guides on how Nature might be turned to Man's advantage in agriculture and navigation, Man became subject to the divine powers of the stars and of astrology. The priests replaced shamans and became specialized interpreters of the divine will. The shamans had operated in a very different society, smaller and more intimate, where consensus was the recognized mode of decision-making. The shaman had to convince others. But the dominance of the priests did not depend on winning agreement from the laity. With larger numbers of people congregated in the community and intimacy in interpersonal communication no longer feasible, the priest became the *de facto* spokesman of that consensus, not one whose authority could be challenged, especially where human sacrifice was the likely penalty for the sacrilegious. So priests, using fear as a religious and political instrument, served in alliance with Rulers to consolidate a regime of Power.

Yet the advance of the Conqueror opened up a new era. The exploitation of natural resources coupled with the exploitation of people, based on the recognition of new divisions of labour, brought into being a period of rapid material development unmatched by anything that preceded it. The Age of Power projected a message that 'might is right'. Morally, Right became redefined by the high priests of Power, so that Might and Right were always in close alliance. Yet even at the high-water mark of Conquest, decay was soon to set in. Conquerors were to find that winning and continuing to exercise Power raised different issues and challenges. The formula that had won success in the past guaranteed neither success nor stability in the future.

Chapter
6

Problems for Rulers

The problem for Conquerors is how to win Power against internal contenders and to exercise it against external enemies until victory is judged to be total. Thereafter the problems change. The Conqueror becomes the Ruler and the principal problem for Rulers is how to administer what has been won. On the surface one might suppose that the life of a Ruler would now be relatively easy. Yet the difficulties faced by the Ruler often prove more challenging than those of the Conqueror. That is because a sharp transition needs to be made between reckless and ruthless enjoyment of the fruits of victory on the one hand and effective pacification of the defeated population on the other. Even when order has been restored, unexpected problems surface and are prone to multiply.

The first step is to reward those who have taken part in the campaign. The Ruler expects to be the main beneficiary from plundering whatever gold, jewels or precious ornaments can be found. But even here difficulties arise, because his generals and lieutenants jealously view what has been won and expect rewards to fit their rank and status. While the aftermath of victory was sometimes genocide, more often the mass slaughter of the defeated would stop at some point. Some defeated males would become slaves. In the earliest days of territorial expansion their numbers were usually few. Slaves were not greatly in demand during early days of territorial expansion for there was not enough routine work other than of a domestic nature to keep them occupied. In any case, men were generally held to make unsatisfactory slaves. Those who begged for their lives, being the most submissive, were judged suitable for enslavement while the rest would be executed.

The next problem to be settled was how to reward the soldiers. Those who had risked their lives in the battle had developed expectations that had to be met if their continued loyalty was to be assured. Foot-soldiers are not in the same position as their commanders, with the means of loading booty that can be carried away. They could stuff whatever they could find into their pockets but in reality there was very little that soldiers could remove without impairing their military capability. But one reward stood as an open invitation. It was inherent in the fact that in any long campaign the men would have been long separated from womenfolk. In the case of mercenaries the licence to rape was part of a widespread, if informal, contract. It would cost the would-be Conqueror nothing. Yet this was the device whereby the extra troops could be raised that could ensure victory.

In the eyes of warrior-victors women were fair game for rape. There was freedom of choice and those who resisted were usually killed. As compliant women were more likely to be spared, natural selection operating over a long period of imperial expansion favoured compliant women. In those cases when a large invading force ultimately withdrew to the home territory, the victors would take some of these women back home with them and the earliest records suggest that women slave-workers played a notable role in making garments. Other slave women were introduced into households as slave-servants and were liable to become concubines. The introduction of slave women into home territory radically changed the stable and long-tested relationship between men and women, which had been such a feature of primaeval society. The significance of the change was that home territory ceased to be the female domain. And so women lost the position that had given them influence over men along with parity of influence they had achieved in the formation of community decisions.

The situation took a new turn when invaders decided to settle permanently in the territories they had won. Then the relationship between the sexes changed even more fundamentally. Wars are inclined to produce a surplus of women in any conquered territory. The greater the scale of the battles fought and the more total the victory, the larger would be the supply of women available to be incorporated into the new society. The effect was that women, rather than being raped and killed, were distributed among the victors in an orderly fashion. Polygamy became the natural consequence of large-scale wars and victories. The Ruler now decided the rules of the game and would lay down how many wives should be allowed for any one man. A favoured number in the Islamic world was four for the rank and file. But, for the Ruler himself, there was no restriction. The number, being infinite, required the setting up of a regulated harem. Power gave the Ruler first choice on the selection of women, which in practice meant those who were physically attractive and virgins. The size of the harem was often a measure of the Ruler's status. Consider the case of Sherifian Sultan of Morocco, Mulay Ismail, who is claimed to have outdone Rameses II of Egypt by begetting 700 sons. Clearly, he must have had very high status.

Many Rulers sought to perpetuate their dynasty by making the fullest use of the harem for the production of sons. Other Rulers, in contrast, had favourite wives, a practice which introduced complications. Wives would then be under-occupied in respect of the sexual activity for which they had been recruited. This failure to match sexual supply and demand meant that the harem was prone to become a centre of intrigue. The most favoured and senior wives of the Ruler tried to reduce its size. Where successful, they brought about expulsion from the harem of those they saw as competitors. These women being granted their 'freedom' were sometimes given gifts as a start to their liberty and to aid their manumission. However, captive women who were released usually had no surviving community to embrace them. Their only means of sustaining themselves economically was by acting as prostitutes in a free market. Another source of outflow from the harem sometimes occurred when a Ruler died and when a successor would be entitled to inherit the harem. However, a not infrequent response was for the son to say, in effect: 'No, I want to create my own harem.' In that event a new exodus of women would add to the numbers of prostitutes and risk flooding the market. Even that means of exit was not available for ageing wives for whom there was no retirement provision. In the case of older or out-of-favour wives of the Ming dynasty in China, they were expelled to work in laundries for the palace beyond the city walls. There they were kept in seclusion under the watchful eye of eunuchs, for it was important to Chinese Emperors that no information of a personal nature should be divulged to the outside world. These expelled wives were fed on rice and salt until 'they died of natural causes'.

The consequence of large-scale warfare in antiquity was to produce a huge surplus of women who were destined to become concubines, wives or prostitutes. The essential difference between an official wife and an official concubine is that only children of the former can stake a claim to inheritance. Concubines and prostitutes have no claim on the men who exploit them. Polygamy, on the other hand, offers a social and political advantage in that it consolidates society. The father of the children becomes a *de facto* member of the family. Conquerors and the subjugated are united in a single community. The Ruler can then supposedly expect loyal support from his extended family and from his many children. Concubines and wives sometimes lived under the same roof in the harem. It is understandable then that many concubines aspired to become wives so that their children might inherit the wealth and position of their father's class. The first step had already been taken by giving birth. Now it became a matter of the next step. In the early Islamic world converting to the religion and beliefs of the father and gaining fluency in the language of the conquerors would advance the cause of the concubine. In the case of Imperial China a somewhat different situation prevailed. There the heir of the Emperor would be the son of a principal wife. Unfortunately there were occasions when a principal wife produced only daughters. That is when a concubine who produced a son might advance her cause. The result was that a principal wife would be demoted and a concubine could then become the new Empress.

Unless the Ruler can solve the problem of inheritance by instituting primogeniture (the oldest son inherits) or a son by a designated chief wife, too many wives produce huge political complications. Two children from different women can be born at approximately the same time and a weakly premature baby might be born minutes before a healthy full-term baby. Some wives might be preferred to other wives and some sons to other sons irrespective of the relationship with the mother. Succession in polygamous marriages was therefore beset with problems. In those relatively few cases where a slave concubine became the favourite of the Ruler and bore him a son, who gained his deceased father's mantle, the outcome was a disaster. A good example was the case of Selim the Sot, the heir of Suleyman the Magnificent and the slave girl Roxelana. Suleyman extended the Ottoman Empire to its furthest limits, almost reaching Vienna. With Selim the Sot, the decline of the Ottoman Empire began. It is a matter for speculation as to what might have happened to Europe had Selim the Sot possessed the same qualities as his father!

The problem of such inheritance was not merely one of overcoming any stigma that might be attached to a slave's son, but that the personal qualities of the offspring often failed to match the general expectations demanded of an heir to empire. In terms of psychobiology such an outcome is hardly surprising. Consider the contrasting situation in traditional societies where in arranged marriages close attention is paid to the family genetic background and the culture that gives it expression. A favoured concubine might be compliant and beautiful but was less likely to pass on the genes that advanced the interests of the Ruler. Every succession in the Age of Power demanded that the heir prove his worth by registering an early victory in the field and extending the empire. The sons of slave women usually proved disappointing in this regard and in consequence were often seen as weak and unfit to rule.

The uncertainties about succession in polygamous marriages meant that if the Ruler did not actively intervene to appoint an heir, fierce struggles took place between the main contenders. The winner would now eliminate all opposition in what was in effect an internal family struggle. So in the case of the Ottoman Empire the triumphant brother would murder all other brothers, a practice which became institutional. These bloodbaths finally became repellent, even by the standards of the Age. Ultimately fratricide was replaced by lifelong imprisonment, a practice known as caging. The story of the Prince of Zenda is held to be an offshoot of that tradition.

The high fertility of Rulers therefore resulted in huge complications where there was no restriction of births in the harems. However, a solution was found. The children of concubines, unlike those of wives, were commonly killed. A harem is designed to be a place where the Ruler can enjoy sexual pleasure undisturbed and there was no intention of allowing children to run around in such an environment. The efficient administration of the harem therefore in operating a policy of ruthlessness became a matter of political importance and required staffing. It was a role for men but not of the normal variety. There were obvious risks in placing fertile and lascivious men in charge of sexually under-occupied and attractive women. The solution, which became standard practice, was to castrate the new guardians of the harem. Such compulsory mutilation was deemed appropriate for slaves but not for members of the Ruler's own tribal group. By this strange route slave eunuchs came to exert increasing power and influence in empire, gradually moving into more administrative roles, including those devoid of any connection with women.

A few women of a vanquished tribe were exempted from being treated as slaves and concubines. It was not uncommon to find the Conqueror claiming the wife of a defeated chief as his own wife. This carried a useful message to the remainder of the vanquished that their former Ruler was now passing on his authority to the new Ruler. Such a marriage was of course political. In the Age of Power many marriages were arranged for political reasons. Different territories could be united through marriage, thus saving the need for a military campaign. However, a Ruler who married with political purpose in mind was more likely to look for concubines with physical and interpersonal appeal. Difficult situations could then arise, for neglect or ill-treatment of a wife would be relayed to the tribe or nation from which she came. So whatever the nature of the Ruler's view on marriage and on the handling of female captives, women caused great complications and problems for Rulers in the Age of Power. The sexual luxury in which Rulers engaged did not reduce their problems but rather increased them.

There were further political problems the Conqueror faced in becoming a Ruler. The assembly of a large fighting force to win territory necessitated ruling peoples whose language the Ruler would scarcely understand and certainly be unable to speak. The

Ruler would be unable to maintain his honoured position through words or force of personality. It would also be difficult to do so by terror alone. Plotting has to be heard and interpreted. Two solutions were available. The first was for all business to be conducted in the language of the Ruler. The easiest method was to appoint members of the Ruler's own tribe to all key appointments. This entourage could also be supplemented with a special police force, drawn from the same band of adherents, and entrusted with identifying and killing all opponents. Ivan the Terrible of Russia developed that facility with ground-breaking refinement. Yet the formula was not foolproof. In a polyglot empire there was always a danger that plots might develop unheeded and unheard among a linguistic minority and grow into open insurrection. A new means had to be found for keeping in close and intimate contact with the varied peoples encased within the boundaries of empire.

In this complicated situation Rulers found that the easiest way of reaching subjects was through religion. Yet one problem had to be overcome. There existed an old, competing, religion based on the world of spirits (animism). Animism, with its vast array of taboos and magic practices and uncontrollable sha-mans, was too chaotic to be sanctioned in an orderly empire and had to be replaced. An orderly empire needs an orderly religion. So a hierarchy of priests was sanctioned with scope to work in whatever language was appropriate in any part of the empire. The role of these priests was to preach an identical religious message that would carry the stamp of imperial approval. The most favoured focus of the new religion lay in the sun and the stars, those markers of the Universe that are comprehensible to all and visible from every corner of the empire. The sun was the giver of life. The stars and their movements charted out the Universe and were already acknowledged as guiding navigators and introducing the sea-sons. In the new religion, the significance of the heavens began to change. Unusual events, as interpreted by the priests, would foretell success or peril in human affairs, including the pro-spects for military campaigns and matters of succession. This gave priests huge scope for influence. So while religion became a unifying force in empire, there was always the danger for the Ruler that religion would get out of hand; that the Chief Priest would become more important and influential than the Ruler. A means had to be found whereby the interests of these two principals could be combined.

The solution was the creation of the god-king. The god-king was of course the Ruler; but it was a Ruler who would be obeyed *because* he was a god. The Incas of Peru, Pharaohs of Egypt, the Dalai Lamas of Tibet and the Emperors of Japan serve as notable god-kings. So holy were the god-kings that only limited contact was permissible with ordinary people. There were other emperors and kings who, while not officially god-kings, were treated in much the same way, being holy and majestic and demanding reverence.

The archetypal god-king had a divine relationship with the stars and would return there on death. In the case of the pyramids of Egypt a small shaft from the inner tomb facilitated passage of his soul to the stars. The Chief Priest acted as his intermediary and on his death would anoint his successor as the new god-king. And so tension between Priests and Rulers was averted because each had a role and a stake in the preservation of the existing order. The danger was that any conspicuous failure on the part of god-king would undermine belief in the official religion and therefore trust in the priests. When such dangers arose, a Chief Priest would sometimes present a restatement of the doctrine that would maintain the credibility of the Faith. Equally, the Ruler could challenge the authority of the Chief Priest as an upholder of the doctrine. If that did not arise, a new Prophet could usurp the function of the Priest and offer a revised doctrine. This independence on the part of religion eventually helped to distance the Faith from the divinity of the god-king. In due course, God, now wrested apart from the person, became an independent divine being. Residing in Heaven, He demanded the same total obedience as the Ruler. His subjects were now obliged to bow down and ask for forgiveness and mercy, which could be granted at the discretion of the priests. So Rulers needed to win approval from priests if their hold on the masses was to be retained. This could present considerable problems for Rulers. However, the formula was still attractive if relations between the Ruler and the masses were to be secured. And so it came to pass that ruthless Rulers saw attractions in the new religion and were 'converted'. The descendants of Ghengis Khan became the Moguls of India and proclaimers of the Islamic faith.

'I think this new religion looks promising.'

All these ramifications in the exercise of Power left untouched a great deal of the social fabric of society, which was able to carry on regardless of the personal identity of the Ruler. What the Age of Power created was a proliferation of ranks and services and new divisions of labour which were no longer gender-related in their arrangement. The whole array of these new positions was male. Such positions multiplied with victory on the battlefield and consolidation of empire. While Conquerors may have been content in their early days to exterminate opponents, Rulers discovered that some of the defeated peoples possessed skills that the victors lacked. Once identified, a professional elite would be relocated to the Ruler's capital, as exemplified in the very thorough actions of Selim the Grim and Kubla Khan in repopulating Istanbul and Xanadu respectively. And so it came about that talented groups or races were settled in ghettos where they contributed to the vitality, economic strength and growth of cities. When these cities were overrun in war, talented craftsmen were relocated again in the service of the new conqueror.

So Rulers learned to hoard talent. Foremost among these regular transferees were the literate classes, among whom the Jews were prominent since literacy was bound up with their

'Scribes, coppersmith and stonemasons fall out. The rest through yonder door.'

religion. While in mediaeval times they were much persecuted, in an earlier period they were given special protection as valued members of the ghetto. Success of empire in gaining riches meant that written records were needed, giving quantities and ownership. The earliest writing related to inventories. Writings of later periods cited the victories of the Ruler. Suitably inscribed monuments added to his preoccupation with prestige. But, in developing written communication, scribes had found a means of communication among themselves, with an inner circle of priests and a small but growing number of lay people. The transition from hieroglyphics to phonetic alphabets threatened to make the illiterate Ruler an outsider, exposing him to the dangers of conspiracy among the literate classes. Should Education be facilitated or opposed? That was the dilemma. The absolute Ruler was doomed whatever the answer. To oppose Education would be to consign the empire to backwardness. To facilitate Education would be to expose the Ruler to the risk of being overthrown by individuals and their entourage, better informed and more knowledgeable; less submissive and more ambitious to exercise their capabilities. As society increased in sophistication, the size of the educated classes grew and the Ruler began to lose his grip.

Chapter

7

The inefficiencies of Power

Power demands control and absolute Power demands absolute control. As Rulers need to exert their control over people, they surround themselves with henchmen on whose absolute loyalty they can count. To this number are added compliant lieutenants who can be relied on to manage the provinces of empire by the standards the Ruler lays down.

While these phenomena are generally acknowledged in politics, they also occur in the management of industrial organizations. The main differences relate to what happens when the wishes of the Ruler are flouted. Absolute Rulers of States take absolute action. Offenders are executed or in other cases assassinated. Potential rivals may be despatched in similar fashion. In the case of industrial empires such extreme actions are debarred. The removal of those who fall from grace is tempered by the existence of Law. Biological life is safeguarded but instant dismissal will terminate the working life of the victim. Humiliated executives are not uncommonly sent home without any previous intimation, never to return again. In all cases, prolongation of the period in Power is liable to diminish the core of people on whom the Ruler, any Ruler, can count as trustworthy confidants. To survive in the inner circle becomes the supreme ambition of supporters. To safeguard their positions and remain close to the Ruler, they will demonstrate loyalty by becoming sycophants.

So established Rulers face a dilemma as their empires increase. Being unwilling to appoint managers with an independent and possibly challenging outlook, they lose touch with the realities of local situations. A gap opens up between what they expect and what actually happens. But who is to pass on the bad news? In ancient times, messengers with bad news risked execution. Even today the risks of showing that the plan has failed are considerable. The safest course is for the news to be distorted and presented in a way that exculpates the entourage of the Ruler. Failings can then be discounted as due neither to misconceptions nor mistaken strategies but to personal faults on the part of those lower down. Rulers and their confidants look for scapegoats. Action taken against scapegoats further publicizes the unchallenged nature of the Ruler's authority and discourages others from going against the Ruler's line. In such a scenario true learning becomes difficult. So the exercise of Power recurringly generates a systems weakness and gives rise to what may be expressed as three Laws.

The First Law
Those who rule by Power become poorly informed and poorly advised and in striving for bigger outcomes are susceptible to making big mistakes.

This First Law applies because it is in the nature of Power to create a structure of command and control that is insulated against feedback. Where no adequate feedback system is operating, ultimate failure becomes only a matter of time.

Now reflect on a second downside in the exercise of Power. The positive aspect of Power lies in its focus on achievement. Power is at its most effective when there is a clear goal in mind and the means for reaching it are already available. That point is often reached without mishap. Then energy, the direction of effort and the ability to command resources produce real benefits. In such a scenario the wielder of Power can often demonstrate a record of achievement that others will fail to match. But consider the case where the means for reaching the goal are not fully developed.

Power on its own achieves nothing without the effective means of delivery. Success will only come about through finding and employing talented people. Yet that is an area where the Ruler is prone to stumble. Talented people are for the most part independently minded and are difficult to manage. Their creativity is curtailed if they are too closely directed. Such a proclivity makes for uneasy working relationships with a Ruler or with the controllers appointed by the Ruler. Talented people may be given limited discretion for a short time. Thereafter impatience and intolerance on the part of their masters rise to the surface and their services are dispensed with. And so a new weakness is revealed.

Second Law
Power will seek but fail to assimilate the highest talent and in rejecting those who possess it will ultimately settle for mediocrity.

Talent is always debatable in terms of where it lies. For one thing, there is no obvious yardstick by which it can be measured. It is not that the Ruler dispenses with the need for talent. Rather it is that the Ruler will choose a human specimen of talent with whom he feels most comfortable. That choice seldom falls on the person whom better informed people will applaud.

Finally, account needs to be taken of what Power sets out to achieve. It is in the character of Power that it feeds on expansion, which becomes a compulsive and never-ending process. The growth of empire places a renewed emphasis on organizational issues and the dilemmas it poses. The wider the domain over which Power operates the more difficult it becomes to combine trust *and* control. Emphasis on securing control lengthens the lines of communication between the apex of Power and its periphery, so creating a lag. Slow responses allow crises to develop that might have been averted given earlier action. But if the emphasis is placed on quicker responses to local crises, new types of organization need to be set in being. In effect locally appointed managers need to be trusted to use their discretion without further reference to higher authority. Such a course of action is possible if Power renounces itself. But then Power ceases to become Power and it would be in the nature of a paradox for Rulers to take such a line. That character flaw gives rise to a further impediment to progress.

Third Law
Power undermines itself through expansion because it can neither tolerate opposition nor empower others.

This Third Law negates the commonly quoted principle that 'success makes for success'. What in effect this Law signifies is that whatever Power may achieve in the short term, it is likely to sign its own death warrant in the longer term. So it may be said that every Napoleon will meet his Waterloo.

The effect of these Laws operating in unison is that the advantages of Power are offset by the severity of its limitations. On the plus side, Power can utilize its strength, based on size and control, to remove both internal and external opposition and sometimes to create a new forward momentum. On the debit side, it is liable to fall behind its smaller, more dynamic and creative competitors. It cannot match them in terms of what it can deliver and the support it can gain from the uncommitted. So the battle scene is set. Power can only continue its reign if it can crush the opposition entirely. Merely to injure the opposition is dangerous, for damaged enemies are created with the incentive to seek revenge. Power can then only safeguard its position by resorting to the cultivation of Terror.

The Age of Power at its zenith established institutions and practices into which atrocities were embedded. Such atrocities need to be distinguished from the modern variants, which tend to be kept hidden, for atrocities in the modern era constitute *bad* publicity. Once reported, the news can be spread around the world fast and excite forces that can be ranged against the perpetrators. But in the Age of Power public atrocities were counted as *good* publicity. Executions were carried out in public and attendance was encouraged.

There is an argument that public executions by hanging or the guillotine are not real atrocities when preceded by judicial proceedings, even if they fail to accord with the accepted canons of civilized behaviour. The same argument may be put forward in connection with public flogging. But public executions and flogging in the Age of Power were often used without reference to Justice as a means of dealing with opponents and in order to instil fear. Heads of executed individuals, placed on spears and displayed prominently, were intended to act as deterrents. In the

'Ill-treat a prisoner in private? You should do it in public, you fool.'

Age of Power at its zenith 'normal' atrocities were not considered atrocious enough. Suffering needed to be maximized. While torture chambers were established with a full range of purpose-designed instruments, they were intended for private victims. Their hidden location, often in dark dungeons, limited their efficacy for producing a public message. More effective in conveying a message was crucifixion, which could be carried out in a public place, typically a hill top, or along public highways, as followed slave revolts. A variant of the public atrocity in other regions of the globe was impaling. Live speared figures were also displayed on highways to gain public attention. The even more painful method was developed of impaling through the anus, a public punishment devised as if for a competition in frightfulness. The public burning of religious heretics brings these displays of public atrocity nearer to our times. The consolidation of these methods for dealing with heresy and insurrection over a long period demonstrates how deeply ingrained was the cultivation of Terror in the Age of Power.

Public atrocities might be reckoned a means to an end and there is no doubt they were. But they were also marks of political systems in decline. A thriving political system is self-regulating and does not need to resort to extreme punishment to enable it to work as intended. Moreover, extreme methods can be counter-productive. The crucifixion of a single person, the long awaited

Teacher of Righteousness, led to a mass moral and religious movement. The meek began to unite and their unity produced a new strength, which the perpetrators of the atrocity and their successors could not resist. To maintain their position, the Sign of the Cross was incorporated in a proclaimed and revised political arrangement. The Age of Power was curtailed to some extent as a result. But its genetic roots remained unmodified, since the leaders of the new religious movement were bachelors and the stock of those who could combine meekness with political ability and leadership declined. In due course meekness lost its momentum as a political force and was overtaken by the forces of Power, now operating in new clothing. Physical atrocities declined in frequency. But *fear* of atrocity in the after-life took its place with depictions of what awaited sinners in Hell. The agony on the Cross now served as a reminder of what pain could be like and reinforced the values inherent in the Age of Power. Submission and confession offered redemption for the loyal and faithful.

Where the Terror and its accompaniment the public atrocity lead to mass revulsion, it becomes inefficient. The reason is that it sets in motion a counter-force that may outplay the forces supporting the Terror. In the short run the contest may be evenly balanced. Its outcome depends on the efficiency of the Terror, which in turn rests on a wide set of prevailing conditions, like the unity of those who enforce it. Yet even if the Terror operates according to plan, there can be no respite from the Laws that continually erode its base and presage its eventual decline.

PART THREE

THE AGE OF ACCOMMODATION

Preview

Once Power ceased to offer evolutionary advantage, many of its features became conspicuously dysfunctional. But fundamental change was slow to materialize. Genetically, society was still made up of the same former people components – warriors, professionals, slaves and primaevals. Centralized bureaucracy replaced and mimicked centralized Power. But while it strove to suppress local democracy, centralized Power, in its emasculated form, began to lose its capacity to control. Printing opened the way to the education and emancipation of the masses and of women in particular. With their starting advantage in communication skills, women were quick to take advantage of newly developing employment opportunities. Politically, women began to exercise their influence away from large groups (dominated by men) and towards smaller, more intimate, teams. As the Age of Power recedes, many of the features of the old primaeval society have begun to reappear both on the political and religious scene and in terms of gender relationships. In this more open society, the genetic roots of behaviour have begun to push through cultural conventions. But in so doing they have created a crisis and a confusion in expectations, as primaeval relationships have clashed with those prevalent during the Age of Power. Amid the coexistence of all intermediate modes of behaviour only prior negotiation about role relationships can introduce a level of stability in the dealings between men and women. Power has fallen increasingly out of favour. On the broader front, leadership is being sought from those who can offer evidence that they are the least likely to abuse it. Such a change in orientation opens the way for decisions in society to be made by larger numbers of locally empowered groups and teams. *Small is beautiful* is on the way back to be reclaimed from its human origins.

8

A change of focus

While Power at its zenith could sweep all before it, victory was never total and absolute for its reach never extended globally. To become Master of the World might be an ambition. But other Power groups occupied other regions of the world and were out of normal reach. Occasionally their oscillating frontiers met. Then one empire would grow at the expense of another so that the situation for any one Power group never remained stable.

All recorded history predominantly revolves round the struggle *for* Power and the struggle *between* Powers. And yet even as great empires jostled for position there were signs that Power was not having a clear run. A new era was ushering in small independent political entities. These might reasonably be termed Refuge States; that is to say there were niches to be found in locations beyond the easy reach of empires, where independent thoughts could safely flourish and where an alternative political formula could be put into action. These Refuge States were mostly islands. Many were islands in the Aegean Sea, like Lesbos, Lemnos and Naxos, which looked to Athens as the largest port in the region. In the Mediterranean, Rhodes, famed for its Colossus (one of the ancient wonders of the world), and Crete, home of the Minoan culture, offered high-water marks for island civilizations, while Venice, one of the smallest states in the world, became in its day the dominating influence of the region. In a later era, empires based on islands offered comparison with mainland empires for the economic and political vigour. The British Empire became physically the largest in the world. Japan was once the strongest power in the Far East and more than a match for China and Russia. In the post-war world Hong Kong and Singapore promoted their economic strength to a level wholly out of keeping with their larger neighbours. But there were other geographical features that could exert the same protective influence as islands. Holland, partly flooded, could produce from its small territory an empire spanning much of the globe. In other instances, mountains offered the same protective benefit as water. Switzerland was established as a sanctuary for refugees from political persecution and also attracted skilled craftsmen from other parts of Europe, so that in spite of its lack of physical resources it was able to combine independence and a high level of economic success. Other thriving locations owed their independence to their location on promontories difficult to reach from the hinterland: some were surrounded by marshes likely to bog down any invading army: while some cities, like Petra and Samarkand, though remotely situated, occupied key positions on trade routes. Often these city-states could not exercise Power because, being small, they could not compete with the land empires. However, the merit of being small made them a less tempting target for expansionists. The strength of such small miscellaneous states resided in the character of their dynamic communities and in particular on a readiness to experiment with different modes of economic activity. Typically they excelled in their understanding and mastery of ships and navigation or in the service they could render to overland travellers on long-distance trade routes.

I have chosen the term Refuge States to underline one feature they all shared. With their wealth depending on trade they had a welcoming approach to visitors, some of whom happened to include political refugees from Empire. Victims of the abuse of Power or those who feared persecution or those who were denied opportunity commonly aspired to relocate there permanently once they had become familiar with local conditions.

Applications for citizenship in the Refuge States were often successful. Regular traders from afar could be assessed by their record and according to whether their skills (and wealth) could enhance the economic strength of the community. So successful cities in protected positions became even more successful through the range of talent they succeeded in attracting and retaining.

'This has been out third good delivery. So I say: how about electing Nauticus a citizen?'

The Refuge States discovered that craft skills and the goods they produced had an export potential, which could be traded for other goods in short domestic supply – a discovery that fostered a mercantile class. As the various cities on the fringes of empires were known for having an oversupply of some goods and an undersupply of others, a role existed for the merchant entrepreneur. The conditions were then created for skilled craftsmen to lay the basis for local industries.

This strategy of drawing in talent had an important bearing on natural selection. Refuge States not only hoarded but they also bred talent. New forms of enterprise and initiative flourished, aided by some of the earliest developments in general education.

In every society some degree of education may be taken for granted, being transmitted by word of mouth or passed on by practical demonstration. In such a way tradition stores and distills past experience and renders it socially available. Yet spoken language as a means of relaying communication through a human chain is subject to one shortcoming: the message can become distorted because memory is both short and imperfect. In this regard Empires took appropriate action in respect of property and the storage of items and in the registering of debt. That is why so much early writing, once deciphered, excites only to disappoint by revealing stock inventories. The other predominant interest of Empire lay in recording the magnificent victories of the Ruler. These were dedicated to impress acolytes but inevitably were less inspiring to the wider world. Beyond these applications, which did not necessitate phonetic writing, Rulers took little interest in the newly developing forms of communication. Instead of promoting new types of economic activity and enterprise, Rulers undertook major projects in building that could act as their monuments and testify to their magnificence. These projects made huge demands on labour and gave rise to wars conducted with the principal aim of supplying slaves. The short-term need had a long-term effect for it changed the demographic composition of empires. Empires now began to contain a relatively high proportion of unskilled workers (slaves) in comparison with Refuge States which continued to foster skills and enterprises of merchants and craftsmen.

Yet the antipathy of Rulers towards literacy eventually weakened. Traditionally Rulers were entertained by bards, for whom the rendering of tales in verse and to a rhythm helped to overcome the problems of memorizing the content. Bards who could recite these tales in full were greatly prized by Rulers for they were part of the luxury of living. Of course Rulers showed no concern for making these stories more accessible to others. But in the Refuge States, already familiar with the use of writing in commercial dealings, its sophisticated population was interested in the use of writing in a *cultural* context. Phonetic writing proved the huge breakthrough, for it meant that stories, poems, history, religious ideas and technological details could equally well be recorded and disseminated as desired. The first phonetic writing, developed in the language of the Refuge State, was a mystery to outsiders, for it was not meaningful in other languages. Empires could not grab the language for their own use even through the exercise of Power, for it was not transferable. Those educated in the language and writing of the Refuge State could communicate with one another and with the *cognoscenti* in other States. Its very secrecy suggested subversion, for neither the Ruler nor the Ruler's spies would know what was being communicated. It is not surprising that book-burning has always been so ardently pursued by the agents of oppression.

Nevertheless, the emergence of phonetic writing and its displacement of cuneiform and other types of writing helped to swing the balance of advantage away from Empires and towards the Refuge States, now taking their place at the forefront of cultural advancement. Their advanced personnel became increasingly sought after in the wider world. They became tutors for the elite and scribes for key administrative roles in the service of Empire. Their mathematicians were indispensable for making calculations and preparing guidelines in the construction of major buildings. While it is the custom of Rulers to set out as would-be Conquerors in the quest for whatever it is they do not possess, there now emerged the great exception to the rule. Refuge States that are the source of valuable personnel cannot be raided and looted in the same way as cities whose wealth comprises material goods. Any such raid might endanger the supply of human talent on which a clear value could now be set. In any case, these Refuge States were often scattered islands, as they were in the prehistoric Aegean. These were sometimes protected by ships that were technically ahead of those of much larger political entities and so could not be suppressed or easily governed. And so Empire began to develop a certain degree of dependency on small but independent nations that existed beyond its borders.

These *external* developments on the fringes of Empire began to limit the omnipotence of Rulers. But now new *internal* factors began to erode their strength. Natural selection had built up Empire on the basis of its twin pillars – aggression and submission. Its key players had both these characteristics. But when aggression becomes detached from submission, dangers arise for Rulers. Embedded in the very extent of Empire was the free rein given to Provincial Governors and to Generals conducting campaigns in distant fields. Moreover, Terror, that trump card that vulnerable Rulers use to reassert their hold on Power, has only limited effects in the longer time. The ultimate riposte is often a backlash fuelled by long festering grudges. So in due course the real threat to Rulers came not from external enemies but from insurrection. Insurrections may be put down, in which case the bloodshed both magnifies the problem and sets in motion damaging after-effects, or the insurrection succeeds and the new Ruler is faced with much the same problems as the old Ruler. Natural selection had brought into being the *masses* who looked for leaders and who were uncomfortable unless they were led. Yet they were others whose allegiance could not be presumed. The behavioural genes of the old primaeval community had never been eliminated but were still pressing for an outlet. They harked back to the caring and sharing society and to primitive communism. They might be cowed by Terror but Terror alienated them from those who imposed it.

There was, however, another way forward. A Ruler's greatest assets lie in the loyalty of his subjects. Loyalty has to be won and retained. The prize for a Ruler in securing loyalty is the prospect of establishing a dynasty so that the loyalty of the masses can be handed on from one generation to the next. The snag, as with a chain, lies in the weakest link. With one bad break in the line, the dynasty is finished. Then the masses seek to transfer their loyalty elsewhere.

It was only a matter of time before the link broke at its weakest point and the dynasty foundered. Then people looked for another form of leadership that could offer continuity and moral security and which could act as a role model. They found it not in the offices of Power but in the teachings and writings of the Prophet. In any long-term struggle for allegiance between a Ruler and a Prophet, the odds are stacked in favour of the Prophet. In so far as the teachings of the Prophet are set down in writing, the continuity of a doctrine is assured and the faith of the faithful can be retained. In contrast, no Ruler can guarantee through a dynasty the perpetuation of his teachings or his charisma. Sons do not necessarily take after fathers and then uncertainty arises. Discontinuity in loyalty to a Ruler has to be set against the continuity and authority of the Prophet's teachings.

The decay of Power as a form of social and political organization was perhaps inevitable in the long run. A single leader exposes a led flock to the inefficiencies that Power introduces and to the injustices that are its hallmark. Yet the concept of Power is deeply ingrained in the human mind, both on the part of those who seek it and those who are subject to it. That is the legacy that natural selection has brought about over a prolonged era. Even if the basis for the prolongation of that era was drawing to a close, humans could not be propelled into the new Age suddenly without an appropriate genetic adjustment. Such a process would require an inordinately long period, even if the requisite conditions prevailed. The only remaining alternative would have been to shorten the journey into a new era by drawing to the fullest degree on insight and education. Continuing external pressure on the frontiers of empire and growing domestic dissension was setting the scene for change. The dissolution of empire was accelerated by the growth of an educational enlightenment that did not properly belong to the Age of Power. A sense of spiritual uplift was being born. Existing institutions could not match the needs of the times. A new era was opening that did not properly fit into either the past or the future.

9

The resurrection of Eve

The Age of Power took away from women all their leading economic and political roles in society. Their greatest source of influence stemmed from marriage into leading circles. But even here marriages were arranged by men, seldom in the search for interpersonal compatibility, more often in order to gain political or financial advantages. Against that general social pattern there seemed little need for that delicate balance in the nature of gender relationships that had evolved throughout the primaeval period.

Yet that transition from the Age of Respect to the Age of Power was not so abrupt as to bring about an immediate change in human behaviour. Natural selection may usher in new inclinations and aptitudes but the older dispositions are not automatically eliminated. There were periods during the Age of Power when gender relationships reverted to a gentler tone, evocative of the Age of Respect. The features of such relationship were most notable among the leisured classes, free from the pressures of the everyday struggle for existence. Such signs could be detected even among the Mogul Emperors, who might well be nominated as being among the world's most powerful rulers. In illustration of the point, Akbar the Great possessed a harem of 5000 women (a figure unsurpassed in my research reading), all of whom were accommodated in palatial surroundings. A contrasting figure was the grandson of Akbar, Shah Jehan, the creator of the Taj Mahal. Generally hailed as the most beautiful building in the world, the Taj Mahal was erected as a monument of his devotion to his Queen, Mumtaz Mahal, who died in childbirth and was esteemed as an exceptionally lovely and cultured woman. Evidently, amid this world of mega-harems, close and sensitive interpersonal relationships between men and women could transcend the brutalities and exploitation that figured so prominently through-out the Age of Power.

Similar contradictions could be noted during the age of chivalry. Brutal wars and struggles between contending parties for advancement in the State did not prevent the emergence of a new respect for women in a context that in itself is revealing. The phenomenon was not widespread in society but mainly confined to the Court. Hence the word *courtship* has entered our language and refers to the delicate early stages of amatory relationships between the two sexes. The man is the suitor and the woman is the responder. Another word significant both for its concept and origins is *courtesy*. A member of the Court would be courteous towards a member of the opposite sex before engaging in courtship or would be courteous as a matter of manners even where no amatory advances were intended. The question now arises: why should this notable elevation in respect for women originate in aristocratic circles?

At this point one needs to bear in mind that a Royal Court comprised people in an especially privileged position. They were free from the pressures of everyday life, they did not need to earn their living and they had plenty of servants to wait on them. To the extent that they kept away from the Affairs of State, the pursuit of leisure now became a principal activity, so allowing them to engage in other types of 'affair'. Flirting, a recognized pastime, was kept within recognized limits out of political necessity. This new focus, safe and yet adventurous, would scarcely have come about were there not a force to drive it. That force could only have emanated from a re-discovery of the basic communication bond that can link men and women. Such relationships had long been driven underground during the Age of Power and yet it was the affluent top layer of society that gave such relationships a new refinement. So the Age of Power produced a small window for the Age of Respect.

That window facilitated a degree of emancipation on the part of women. One of the earliest of the Court women to become emancipated was Christine de Pisan, who was born in Venice in 1363.

Although an Italian by birth, she was French at heart as well as in education and fame. When she was five years old she went to Paris with her father, Thomas de Pisan, who had been appointed astrologer and secretary to King Charles V. She was reared at the court, and educated in the ancient languages and literatures. At the age of fourteen she married a nobleman from Picardy, and, when her husband died, she was only twenty-five years old and had three children to provide for.

She decided to earn her income as a writer. Her poems, songs and ballads were well-received and soon she was able to support her family. Christine de Pisan became popular and her work was later supported by many lords and ladies of medieval Europe, to which may be added King Charles VI, and his wife Queen Isabella of Bavaria. Much of her work contains a great deal of autobiographical information, unusual for writers of that time, but in the main comprises poems, allegorical tales, moral philosophy and commissioned biographies.

Christine de Pisan was very devoted to France and was horrified by the civil strife that erupted after the assassination of Louis of Orleans. In 1410, she wrote Lamentations on the Civil War, *and then* The Book of Feats of Arms and Chivalry, *which was one of the first books by a woman to be translated into English. She was devastated by the hostilities with England and the Hundred Years War and, in 1418, she retired to live in a convent.*

The tendency for a Court elite to elevate the meaning of love and thereby to raise the status of women had however only limited consequences. Most women of the period who achieved distinction in their own right owed their position to the early death of a reigning King. Nevertheless they were memorable for being set in an era when opportunities for women were negligible or non-existent. But in themselves such examples did not presage an opening of the doors to allow an onrush of women to burst through the barriers of gender restriction. In general, women were confined not by technical barriers but by their social position. Yet it was a technological development, that at the time must have been assessed as gender-neutral, which eventually had such huge repercussions. That event was printing. Yet for a great span of time printing was an entirely male business, created to serve male interests, and it was only at a much later date that the progressive development of printing precipitated an unforeseen social revolution.

Here it is useful to make a résumé of what happened. The first printers of whom we have knowledge were the early Egyptians. The print they used is evidenced by inscriptions on bricks and requires a hard material to be pressed against a softer. Some of the stamps they used for the purpose now form part of the antiquarian treasures of the British Museum. Similarly stamps were used in the striking of coins so that the invention of money created another forward step in the art of printing. However, true letter-press printing requires the transfer of ink and necessitates a different type of technology. The first recorded invention is attributed to Foong-taon, a minister of state in China in the tenth century. Being a learned man, as all great officers of state in China needed to be, he desired to multiply the copies of a book which pleased him, and at the same time save the labour of writing them. His accomplishment was to place a wet page written in ink upon the face of a smooth piece of wood. The wood untouched by the ink was cut away to form an engraved tablet. That engraved tablet once wetted with ink could transfer its impressions on to a page of blank paper. In the thirteenth century Marco Polo returned to Venice with news that the Chinese were using printed paper money. That news stimulated interest in this area and soon led to the printing of playing cards to amuse King Charles VI. The next development in printing involved the use of wooden letters of the alphabet which could be put together in a frame to form a printing plate. But wooden letters soon wore out so that any printing run would be limited. The real breakthrough, which was to have such important consequences, occurred in the middle of the fifteenth century. John Guttenberg from Germany worked in Holland as an apprentice of Coster, a well-established printer, who used wooden-type letters. Guttenberg is alleged to have stolen some wooden letters during Coster's temporary absence from the premises and to have returned to his home town, Mentz, where he set up a similar business which he then proceeded to develop. The importance of Guttenberg lies in his invention of printing letters *made of metal* and the invention led to the printing of the famed Guttenberg bible. While John Guttenburg established the technical means for the mass printing of books, he declined to reveal that his copies of the bible were actually *printed*. Instead they sold as expensive hand-written copies. One of his customers, the Archbishop of Paris, being greatly impressed, showed his copy to the King, only to discover to his shock that the two copies were identical in every detail. So in 1462, believing this conspiracy to be the work of the devil, Archbishop Adolphus sacked the city of Mentz. The printing trade of the place was thereby ruined and the workmen dispersed in search of a livelihood. Thus the art of printing that had been so carefully concealed rapidly spread to other parts of Europe.

That single invention of Guttenberg was to have a remarkable impact on the status and eventual emancipation of women. A perspective on its general effects is well described in an early history of printing, published in 1855 by the Society for the Promotion of Christian Knowledge, in the following terms:

> *Before the invention of the art, the great body of people in every country was sunk in ignorance. Learning was confined to a few persons; and these, if they had the inclination, had not the means of diffusing it. The poorest man in the present day is in a better position, in this respect, than the richest man was before printing had been discovered. The poorest man may now obtain the books which kings and princes and learned men once counted amongst their richest possessions. The poorest man may now store his mind with the best thoughts of the best minds of all ages; for printing has placed all learning within the reach of almost all sorts and conditions of people. Printing has enabled men to instruct themselves in the ways of wisdom, both human and divine; to make knowledge serve them in earning their daily bread; and to enjoy in their leisure one of the most innocent of human pleasures.*

Before the printing of books all trades and professions involving reading or writing were monopolized by men. The effective restriction of a trade or profession to one gender is bound to convey the general impression that the excluded gender lacks the aptitude for that occupation. That position then becomes self-perpetuating. However, cheaply produced books left around in the household invite curiosity. Once the phonetic nature of the alphabet was understood it was easy for women who spent so much time in the house to teach themselves to read. Reading stimulates the thirst for knowledge. And knowledge fuels ambition to use what has been learned.

There are some occupational activities that are clearly gender-related, for genetic rather than for cultural reasons. Hunting and tool-making are the prime examples and have their roots in the long primaeval period when physical characteristics played such an important part in the distribution of roles between men and women. Reading and writing had no primaeval roots and therefore might be considered gender-free. On the other hand these arts might be considered as the ultimate outgrowth of the human desire to communicate. Once reading and writing had been invented, women showed a particular aptitude in that direction. Not only are women keen communicators but the foundations for the aptitude to read and write may have been laid by their capacity in other activities. It is evident that they were capable of making fine discriminations as domestic gatherers of plants and fruit in the primaeval period and in the stitching of clothing. Those foundations were furthered demonstrated as women distinguished themselves as artists in embroidery and makers of tapestries in mediaeval times. Letters of the alphabet need fine discrimination in their perception, while quickness of response aids speed of reading. It is interesting to note that present-day girls commonly outstrip boys in achieving the standard laid down for reading in the early stages of schooling.

To the powers that be, the printed word must have seemed little more than a variant of the hand-written word except in relation to the economics of production. But there was one important difference in terms of its social consequences. Printed literature can find its way into any quarter, including a lady's bedchamber. Early printed literature was often seen as subversive because it would end up in the hands of those who were not 'supposed' to see it. Printed books deprived the elite of their monopoly over knowledge but also opened up competing forms of knowledge and philosophy to a wider population. Once these 'risks' were perceived, book-burning became the hallmark of tyrants. Women were not reckoned as being subject to these risks. The presumption must originally have been that it would not have any bearing on women's interests or attitudes. After all, women were illiterate. They could scarcely have been otherwise, for scribes and clerks belonged to a wholly male occupation, and education was directed towards those who would benefit from it occupationally.

'So what's this you've brought home?' 'It's a book.'

But once books had been published and found their way into the home, a new situation arose. Books were now there to be investigated and studied by women with leisure time on their hands. Women needed only to tease out from men what the letters of the alphabet meant. The phonetic roots of words enabled them rapidly to deduce the meaning of all that was printed. So women, though denied education, 'discovered' reading and writing. As soon as they did so, the flood gates opened and the pressures to become educated began. Education, including self-education, meant that occupations originally conceived as male preserves now became subject to pressures from women demanding the right of entry and equal treatment.

Universal education has played a major part in advancing the position of women in the Age of Accommodation. But it is not the only factor. The changing nature of work has been another. Industries that depended on brawn (in their early days), including coal, shipbuilding, steel manufacturing and heavy engineering, have declined. Their place has been taken by an upsurge in light industries, requiring faster work and the handling of smaller items. Computer applications entail the reading of fast-moving screens and the rapid tapping of keyboards. Much business communication now takes place on the telephone and demands interpersonal skills in conversation. All these changes have shifted the balance from the dominance of men in gainful occupations to a more even employment spread between the two genders. Notably in those regions where the greatest shifts have taken place, the employment balance has tilted in the reverse direction from that which formerly existed. The new jobs have created more opportunities for women than for men. The main limiting factor to these take-ups have been child-bearing and the upbringing of young children. So the advancement of women poses for them a new dilemma – how to balance their career expectations with their personal life.

10

The genetic legacy

The extinction of human populations has become less common-place in the last two thousand years. For some thousands of years before that there was nothing extraordinary in one group of people setting out to exterminate another. That, as was mentioned earlier, was the recorded fate that befell the unfortunate Hittites, Amorites, Caananites, Perizzites, Hivites and Jebusites. Extinction played a major part in sharpening the genetic differences between survivors and non-survivors and in speeding up human evolution in terms of psychogenetic characteristics and their cultural concomitants. But with the eventual demise of the god-king as the central figure in nation-states, the situation changed. Genocide, as standard practice, went into decline. One reason was connected with the rise of universal religions, like Christianity and Islam, and world religious and secular philosophies that included Buddhism, the Bahai Faith, Taoism and others. Any creed that embraces adherents from different races cannot sanction genocide. The sharp fall in genocide has been a factor in the rapid rise in the population of the world. Killing of course continued as nations fought nations. But the issues were primarily about political control, doctrinal disputes or economic rivalry and in most cases had limited biological significance. Victors and losers would suffer fatalities, sometimes on a large scale, but their genetic stock continued largely unchanged.

Our distance from pre-history and from the beginnings of historical records causes one to lose sight of that era and to underestimate the magnitude of the evolutionary changes that took place and which affect us so much today. The extent of the change can be summarized as follows. The Age of Power *selected out* those personal attributes of character and behaviour that belonged to the Age of Respect and offered no survival value. The earlier focus on harmony in the community and with Nature offered no competitive advantage in the eventual struggle for territory. Primaeval people had a balanced life-style: they worked for their living when they needed to and, unless the food supply ran out, they had ample time for leisure. It was a formula for contentment but not for change. Evolution continued to move slowly until competition for territory generated a new challenge. The Age of Power now took a new turn in that it *selected in* aggressive and destructive qualities (on the male side). Primaeval and peaceful people were pushed aside in favour of a new breed of successful Warriors whose orientation was to win territory by defeating other males. These Warriors operated in large bands and were strongly bonded to their fellow Warriors. Absence from womenfolk of their own kind brought in its wake sexual deprivation. Such abstinence would be endured even for long periods but only for an eventual reward. In the end that reward grew into a genetic appetite to rape women, an opportunity always on offer as a consequence of victory on the battlefield and the slaughter of the opposing males. Warriors needed leaders and, unlike Primaevals, they aspired both to lead and to be led. They and their kind were always locked in struggles either with outsiders or, when external enemies were absent, with insiders in a struggle for dominance.

The success of Warriors on the battlefield eventually brought into being subject people whose continued survival depended entirely on the whims of their captors. Enemies who prostrated themselves and begged for mercy and showed humility towards their captors were most likely to be spared. Cruel Warriors often revelled in tormenting and humiliating those they had con-quered. Defeated populations gradually became transformed in character as a result of natural selection. Those who resisted their overlords were exterminated, while the survivors were predominantly those who accepted subjugation under the Ruler. The most extreme were the anxious 'submissives', ever-ready to plead for forgiveness and pardon. Such 'submissives' needed to play out their humility and, in so far as they were exempted from work on behalf of the Ruler, they gravitated to isolated religious establishments where they could pray in peace, undisturbed by potential threats from the outside world. At one time monasteries, and similar establishments housing submissives, were widely distributed around the world. In due course these spared victims of the Age of Power along with their genetic descendants have become fewer, and inevitably so, since they did not constitute a breeding population. In retrospect, it might be claimed, they embodied the Age of Respect and with their passing the world has become less respectful.

Submissives for the most part escaped being made slaves, because they owed their lives to the whims of the Conqueror rather than depending on his intention to find supplies of labour. The need to find worker-slaves followed a different route. As the powerful became more ambitious and conceited, they demanded ever-larger buildings to reflect their status. Megaliths, great temples and large fortifications demanded huge amounts of labour. That is why slaves figured conspicuously in almost every ancient empire and in the more recent opening up of the Americas.

From the point of view of law and of Human Rights, slavery is regarded as a single entity and indeed as an abomination. But from the point of view of the genetic legacy, important distinctions need to be made between different classes of slavery. Some slave populations, perpetuated in their original locations, were ethnic groups overrun by invaders and kept in a state of subjection. The helots of ancient Sparta and the Untouchables of contemporary India offer examples. The genetic legacy of such populations did not change further as a consequence of their continuing subjugation.

A second group of slaves were the product of fierce struggles between nations or cities. The men, women and children of the losers were 'sold into slavery' and transported to any destination in which buyers were to be found. Commonly men were separated from women, being required for different purposes.

Hence the stock of the defeated population no longer continued as a distinct breeding group.

An eventual thriving market for slaves created two types of supplier: professionals and amateurs. Foremost among the former were Arab slave-traders who could provide a regular service and on whom, for example, the explorer and missionary Livingstone relied to convey his post and supplies in their returning trip from the coast. Professional slave-traders supplied selected slaves, including both men and women, to a discerning slave market and I will refer to these as A-class slaves. However, the eventual boom in slave-trading created another type of supplier – opportunist amateurs who would round up primitive communities and ship them in bulk to a slave market. These I will refer to as B-class slaves. I do not believe these latter slaves had any distinguishing characteristics as potential workers. Their only evident feature is that they were less able to resist better-armed slave-traders. On the African continent it seems that many B-class slaves were taken from aboriginal-type communities. With their easy-going life-style 'primaevals' were unlikely to make good worker-slaves. And so a mixture of slaves came on to the slave market with both A-class and B-class slaves being supplied.

Slave-traders made a profit from selling slaves with the consequence that, from the viewpoint of the slave-owner, the cost of slaves was not negligible. For a time, slave-owners sought to buy only male slaves to work their estates. Many slaves, being ill-treated, ran away if they could, so that the investment on the part of the slave-owner was lost. In Roman times absconding slaves who were caught were branded, which discouraged escapes. But in America comparable punishments were less effective. Runaway slaves often escaped to cities or the remote countryside often with impunity. With the passage of time slave-owners and slave-traders came to recognize that 'good' slaves were an investment that could offer a long-term return. Selected slaves were therefore afforded access to women. These were supplied not out of the kindness of the slave-owners' hearts, but because there was an economic advantage in producing a continuous supply of first-class slaves. So worker-slaves gave rise to procreating-slaves, singled out for their brawn, their robust good health, their readiness to engage in arduous physical labour and their respect for firm authority.

Such A-class slaves, supplied by professional slave-traders for a discerning slave market, I have called True Slaves. Domestic slaves were entirely selected from this category, just as they were in Roman times. In psychogenetic terms, such slaves should be seen as distinct from B-class slaves who possessed little merit from the point of view of the slave-owner.

'The price of a good slave is getting outrageous.'

Once slavery was abolished in America, many Blacks failed to earn a living in a free labour market and congregated in urban areas where they formed part of a growing underclass. An underclass comprises those who no longer seek employment in the formal labour market. As their number grows, they form an underclass culture with values of its own and a social acceptance of crime. A parallel trend among the dispossessed and the detribalized emerged in Australia and in many urban areas of

Africa. This whole field, and how it should be approached, is fraught with controversy. Education has been hailed as an answer to these problems. Even Headstart (a programme of cultural enrichment) in America has failed to provide a solution. In Australia and in some immigrant areas in the United Kingdom educational attainment, on the basis of measured performance, has fallen far short of expectation. That failure of education to deliver has been alleged as due to the 'racism' of teachers. Yet for those who have studied primaeval communities there should be nothing surprising about such disappointments among some groups. Aborigines lead a relatively carefree life without the achievement-orientation and specific cognitive abilities that characterize some other peoples and their descendants are unlikely to differ appreciably. In Australia the sheer size of the outback has enabled aborigines to rediscover their culture in areas undisturbed by Whites. The success of this alternative strategy is becoming increasingly recognized, especially in the Northern Territories. In America the abortive attempt to pursue educational and employment 'equality' in the crime belts of urban cities has given rise to a policy vacuum with no alternative strategies in place for those who find themselves separated from their natural habitat and in a downwards spiralling plight.

Slavery is a recent phenomenon in historical memory in some parts of the world. Elsewhere, while slavery was once widespread, it has long since been abolished as a social practice. But that is not tantamount to saying that slavery has been abolished genetically. In Europe, when slavery was largely brought to an end about two thousand years ago, the direct consequence was that, under feudalism, True Slaves were transformed into serfs. Serfs belonged to their Masters, in so far as they were tied to the land their masters owned, and were required to render to their masters a proportion of all they produced. The essential difference was that their Masters relinquished power over life and death that they had wielded over slaves. Hence while 'natural selection' had operated rigorously in respect of True Slaves, it no longer applied to serfs. But by then the gene pool had stabilized. Serfs for the most part inherited the genetic characteristics of True Slaves. In the same way their successors, peasants, inherited the same characteristics as serfs. Peasants as freemen now owned their own plots of land, enjoying improved conditions of life and different types of social relationship. Yet in spite of these changes they still sprung from the same stock as procreating slaves and serfs and showed the same genetic capacity for hard physical work as their forebears. So, while this evolving history of manual workers covered an extensive period, it is important to remember that 'natural selection' was exercising its effects very vigorously at the beginning of this historical process rather than during the intermediate or later stages. In the era when slavery was at its height the evidence from the period suggests a preponderance of A-class slaves. That this should be so is understandable. When ruthlessness reigned and was free from curbs, A-class slaves made a better proposition than B-class slaves. That distinction became important for subsequent generations.

While slavery has left its considerable mark not only on history but on the biological stock of those who have sprung from that era, another group of people with distinctive genetic features evolved in the Age of Power. These were the Professionals. By this term one refers to the wide range of craft-workers with useful aptitudes and refined skills, on which the prosperity of cities and nations rested. Large projects could not be successfully under-taken and completed without their help. They were therefore assiduously sought after, selected and enlisted in the service of ambitious Rulers. These elite workers, set up in ghettos and given special protection and privileges, were always male, with part of the deal being the inclusion of their womenfolk in the ghetto. True Professionals therefore became, like True Slaves, a distinctive breeding group.

So, to summarize, during the Age of Power men were selected for their special characteristics – Warriors for their fighting qualities, Slaves for their capacity for hard physical work and acceptance of authority, and finally Professionals for their superior skills and talents. Other people who were overrun during the Age of Power were killed or allowed to perish or they survived only in greatly reduced numbers. Many perished for indirect rather than direct reasons due to the failure of indigenous people to resist germs, such as measles and smallpox, brought in by invading Warriors. Sometimes germs have aided indigenous peoples to resist invaders, especially in respect of tropical diseases. In such cases would-be Warriors have withdrawn from prospective settlement. As a result indigenous peoples have only had their own more locally based Warriors with whom to contend. But where invading Warriors have become settlers, natural selection through disease has speeded up the extinction of earlier populations. Paradoxically, the proneness of Warriors to rape the females of conquered indigenous people has to some extent aided the genetic survival of a conquered race. Half-castes have benefited by being immune to the introduced diseases and have therefore been more easily assimilated into the culture of the Conquerors.

While the nature of natural selection, as it pertained to men, has operated on distinctive lines throughout the Age of Power, the evolutionary process has followed a different course in relation to women. Women have not been selected for their abilities throughout the struggles of history but for their readiness to entertain and serve men. In short, women have been selected for their beauty and their submissive sexual and social behaviour. On such a basis gender differences were consolidated and Rulers fully expected that they would be self-perpetuating. Given consistency in the pattern of social policies over a vast period of time, one might even suppose that the evolutionary process would widen these differences in the ability of the two genders. In other words, men would end up as a result of natural selection processes with an advantage over women in ability.

There are, however, reservations about accepting what seems a persuasive, if simplistic, line of argument. *Some* abilities, based on aptitude and interest, are clearly gender-related. For example, tool-makers and tool-designers have been almost exclusively male from the earliest times to the present day, while the nurturing occupations have been mainly female. But does this mean that *most* occupations are necessarily gender-related? An alternative possibility is that while *some* occupations are gender-related, good performance in other occupations depends more on basic ability than on gender. In that case a different set of questions present themselves. Is basic ability inherited so that it will surface in both men and women in roughly equal measure but will take on different forms according to gender-related aptitude? Aptitude depends on a combination of ability and interest. For any given occupation people need both if they are to perform well. So is it not possible that humans have genetically transmitted abilities and gender-specific aptitudes? Given a wide enough choice in occupations, together with the freedom to decide, men and women can be expected to arrive in the occupations that most appeal to their respective gender providing the culture allows it.

Throughout the Age of Power that range of possibilities never operated. The belief was deeply ingrained that men were better fitted for the more demanding jobs because they had more *general* ability. In retrospect, that outlook was clearly a departure from the views prevailing in primaeval society. Nor was it a view that could be readily verified or refuted, for there were no cross-gender occupational movements. Submissive women, selected for beauty or sexual compliance, were in the spirit of the times denied any leading economic or political position. The dogma about gender differences had been taken so far that its faults were often exposed. Sons were supposed to take after their fathers. And yet there were conspicuous episodes where this failed to happen, especially when men consorted with those outside a favoured genetic pool. For example, it was commonly observed that a Ruler who married outside his class or bore a bastard would be disappointed to find his son showing a lack of dedication to military training and being drawn instead to artistic pursuits, the pursuit of pleasure or religious piety. Conversely, the feminine kin of powerful Rulers often behaved in ways that reflected their father's attributes rather than those usually associated with women. Potential queen-mothers, being ambitious for their sons in the race for succession, had no compunctions against poisoning competitors. But even the most notorious women in history hardly bore comparison in ruthlessness with the most ferocious men. In general, in spite of a few cross-gender movements, recorded usually as oddities and exceptions, the gap in gender roles remained wide. Men displayed male characteristics and engaged in male occupational roles involving high office, while women stayed in the ancillary roles to which they had been assigned and for which they were judged best suited.

Notions of genetic inheritance were often crude. For example, one theory was that bone was inherited from men (that is the harder and more robust qualities) and blood from women (that is the softer and weaker parts). Men were wise and decisive and women weak and vacillating. Transgender transmission did not occur to people. Understandably, Education was confined to men. It was held that, if women lacked the basic ability to profit from Education, time and effort would be wasted in educating them. Such views prevailed for a very long time. And then cross-gender transmission was seen as a real genetic possibility. Bernard Shaw is famed for bringing the issue into the public arena. Shaw was once propositioned by a woman offering to bear him a child, on the grounds that such an offspring would possess both brains and beauty, Shaw replied: 'Madam, he would probably have my looks and your brains.'

Shaw's admirer clearly had views in line with mediaeval patriarchs who had no clear pragmatic information on which to base their opinions. Such patriarchs would be flabbergasted by the outcomes of the present day when girls and boys have received education on equal terms. Rather than confirming the wisdom of channelling educational resources towards boys as the better investment, the facts could easily be interpreted as pointing in the opposite conclusion. The current position is that girls are inclined to read and write more quickly than boys. Girls are now moving on to higher education in larger numbers than their male counterparts. It has been estimated that they are currently taking twenty per cent more university places than would be justified on gender equity in the countries of the European Union. Such a trend has an important bearing on employment. Of the new jobs being created in the labour market, the greater proportion is being filled by women rather than by men. It is as though the pattern of history in occupational terms is now standing on its head. What explanation could possibly be offered to our mediaeval patriarch?

We would first need to correct his views about the inheritance of characteristics. One would not dispute that important differences exist between the orientation of men and women. But it would have to be pointed out that temperament and abilities should not be treated as though they were one and the same. What would need to be emphasized is that *general ability* can have outlets in many different directions. Our medieval patriarch might well be conscious of this variability in relation to men but less aware of it in relation to women, whose abilities were always seen in a very restricted context.

The fact that there might be a problem about how to impart the notion of the cross-gender transmission of general ability is hardly surprising. The subject only came to the fore through the development of modern psychology. One of the early pioneers in the study of ability was Spearman. He was able to show by statistical analysis that most abilities are compounds of general and specific factors. The general factor relates to general intelligence or G, as he described it. G relates to the tendency for individuals to perform generally well or generally badly over a wide range of different tests. However G also needs to be understood in relation to S. S refers to a specific aptitude. A cluster of S scores may be an indicator of G but any one particular score may be unrelated. In other words, some people will prove able at most things, while others may prove able in only a single activity. Now it seems that G is subject to cross-gender inheritance but S is less so. A highly intelligent scientific instrument-maker may have a highly intelligent daughter, but she is unlikely to have an equivalent aptitude for, nor an interest in taking up, the occupation of her father. It is far more likely that she will display her talents in other directions. If men have an S in relation to tool-making and tool-design and the design of advanced engineering systems, women have an S in relation to communication. Such an aptitude has a deep-rooted biological basis. Mothers have always played a crucial role in teaching babies to articulate and young children to speak. Men are more concise in language: chatting disturbs animals, being a liability in the hunt.

However, oral communication is only one form of communication. The development of printing opened up new vistas of communication based on the printed and later the written word. Women moved in large numbers into clerical and secretarial work. And as women became emancipated through further education, their interest in interpersonal communications found new outlets in a range of occupational activities. In the contemporary world women not only have a major share in the 'primaeval' caring and nurturing occupations but have entered in increasing numbers into the better paid jobs of public relations, journalism, computer-related jobs involving word-processing and the many occupations covered by 'the media'.

General ability does not advertise itself in the same way as physical inheritance with its evident visibility. General ability can only be inferred and that is no doubt why it can take so long to recognize. But ability is not the only invisible factor operating. There is a third factor in the equation – temperament. In the modern world, people with the benefits of experience in making placements focus increasingly on having the 'right temperament for the job'. Temperament is genetically rather than culturally determined and subject to the forces of evolution and natural selection.

Selection for temperament is well borne out in the animal-breeding world. For example, Rottweilers have a notorious reputation as fearsome guard dogs. However, some pet owners claim that *their* Rottweiler is a wonderful dog with children and has a 'sweet disposition'. Put photographs of the two Rottweilers side by side and it is doubtful that anyone could tell which was which. A dog breeder would know from *the record* because pedigrees are preserved and extensively studied. The difference between dogs and humans in terms of their lineage is that dogs are bred *purposely* and in a controlled way, while humans breed at something close to genetic random. Dog breeders have a better understanding of breeding than Rulers.

It is true that Rulers have shown an incidental, and perhaps unconscious, appreciation of the subject by collecting people in ghettos. This was a policy that led to the creation of a particular ability gene pool. The policy was devised in respect of men and its effects spread, in an unsuspected way, by cross-gender transmission to women. However when one moves from ability to temperament a different set of forces have operated on outcomes. The agents of Evolution have been primarily Conquerors rather than Rulers and the objects of that transmission have been women rather than men. Women have received *some* cross-gender transmission of temperament through their genetic relationship with Warriors. But the more *direct* inheritance of temperament has come as a consequence of natural selection where women have been the victims of conquest. Through the prolonged Age of Power warfare led to a surplus population of women and, as noted earlier, those who survived had to overcome the hurdle of rape. Warfare and rape were interlinked. Wars take men away from women. Mercenaries in particular make a choice: they can stay at home with their womenfolk or they can depart on an expedition where the only incentive is to avail themselves of the booty that follows victory. Some of that booty relates to material goods. But there will not be much that foot-soldiers can carry away with them on their person. The other promise is sexual licence with women of the defeated. That offer was made quite explicitly by would-be Conquerors and fully understood by troops. So for men who made that choice, in preference to staying with their womenfolk, rape would be the more attractive proposition. In that way the genetic susceptibility to rape was established among large numbers of Warrior men.

Persistent rape over a huge time-span has had significant genetic effects. Rape has severe emotional consequences for most women. Almost certainly in terms of Evolution a distinction needs to be drawn between those who resisted in defence of their honour (and were likely to be killed) and those who submitted. Here a certain amount of speculation is inevitable, for there is very little direct evidence from history. Women subject to such ordeals do not keep diaries. However, journalistic reporting of mass rape in modern warfare during the twentieth century offers some testimony. When the Red Army first entered Germany at the conclusion of the last war, many women are recorded to have committed suicide, notably by drowning themselves in lakes, rather than submit to mass rape. Many have been killed by invading armies as the price of sexual resistance. Recurring incidents in contemporary society tell a similar story. Unaccompanied women have been attacked, raped and killed as they made their way home at night. But there is also scattered testimony about survivors. Some women have fostered the illusion in their attackers (to which rapists seem prone) that their victims have enjoyed the experience. A future meeting has been arranged at which the police have been called and so by that cool ruse rapists have been entrapped. Many women do not even report rape and incidents are revealed only at a later date. It appears that the most passive and asexual have the best chance of surviving rape. Now if such a distinction between victims and survivors is multiplied by the experience of many centuries, it can be inferred that women who were submissive had a distinct advantage in the event of territorial invasions. In other words, temperamental submissiveness favoured survival and equipped such survivors for passive occupations, often deemed 'women's work'.

However, submissiveness is not the universal female legacy. While Warrior Men selected for themselves submissive women, or enforced submission by acting as the *paterfamilias* in a truly patriarchal culture, they also generated a caste of their own, marrying into the kin of other Warrior Men. The aggressive streak of the Warrior would almost inevitably be transmitted to their daughters. By taking after their fathers rather than their mothers, they produced a new breed of Warrior Women.

Now consider the third group, Professionals. These are the descendants of those whom the Conqueror selected and the Ruler protected on account of their superior trade and literary skills. Such people, as we have seen, were always male. But because of the inheritance factor in respect of general ability, they produced a new line of able women. These were well placed to take advantage later of the new professions suited to the intrinsic skills and abilities of their sex. Professional Women, just like Professional Men, are genetically equipped to prosper in the new conditions created by the Age of Accommodation.

So Evolution has bequeathed over a vast passage of time four prime groups – the Primaevals, the Warriors, the Slaves and the Professionals. Genetically, we may ask: where are they now? The answer is: they are still with us. The genes have not changed but the conditions and the culture have in an increasingly cosmopolitan world. There has been some genetic migration with each group losing some of its purity. While cities may have been founded on ghettos containing segregated communities, in due course ghetto and class boundaries began to break down and intermarriage stretched across our four prime groups. Even so, people still have acted as though all the significant characteristics were transmitted through the male line. Genealogy provides a case in point. Genealogy focuses on tracing the family, i.e. male, surname. To subject the female line to the same scrutiny would entail a great multiplication of genealogical research activities. Most families who take their past seriously would have to accept that in genetic terms they would soon lose track of where they stood. Our four prime archetypes will probably cover only a minority of the total population, although I have often found individuals stand out as good exemplars of one prime group. But hybrids between these four groups, as a result of intermarriage, are more common than the prime types themselves. I have set out below the distinguishing features of these archetypes and their hybrids as they relate to mature adults and the most active players in contemporary society.

While I believe I have set out the principal archetypes that represent the mainstream of psychogenetic inheritance in the human stock, I concede there are other legacies. The Age of Migration produced and rewarded psychogenetic 'explorers', that is to say those who were disposed to look forever beyond the horizon and wonder what was there. It was the sort of wonder that led to wander. In terms of psychology it is recognized as the Peer Gynt syndrome. In earlier times the phenomenon had an important part to play in spreading humans to all parts of the globe. Earlier in this chapter I have given attention to 'submissives' and to B-class slaves. It is only

Genetically driven behavioural archetypes as manifested in contemporary society

Note: Genetically driven behaviour refers to behaviour that persists irrespective of cultural norms or personal pressures. Such behaviour is the end-result of the complex interactions of the evolutionary process. Some people will behave true to type in relation to the prime factors that have moved evolution forward while others exhibit hybrid behaviour.

These 'true' models relate to how that behaviour might appear at the present day. The hybrid behaviours relate to crosses between two parent types. It is a genetic principle that crosses can produce both the best and worst features of the genotype. Both are given in the case of the hybrids.

Male True Primaeval	Female True Primaeval
Likes to balance earning a living with leisure. Finds routine work a burden. A 'spontaneous' approach to life. Keen on hunting or fishing or voyaging in boats or cars. Likes time off 'with the boys' or spending time in men's clubs. Admires male sporting heroes as role models. Yet at home relies on wife or partner for support and a wide range of personal services. Respects her authority in the household. Strives to please her but insists on keeping his leisure pursuits. Sexually well adjusted in relation to primaeval woman. Likes spontaneous music and dance. A devotion to 'green' issues.	A good homemaker, interested in furnishing and decorating the home, in fashion, in hairstyling and in wider family. Nurtures plants in garden or home. Likes shopping and 'gathering' in supermarkets. Loses her way outside local environment, where she prefers partner to drive car. Avoids competing with male roles. Believes in letting men 'do their own thing'. Cultivates close friendships with other women. Looks after the wider family. Sexually well adjusted. A 'spiritual' approach to religion.

Male True Warrior	Female True Warrior
Aroused by physical challenge and sense of competition. Interested in weapons and history of warfare. Prone to violence if provoked. Hostile to or suspicious of outsiders or foreigners. Loyal to chosen male in-group. Ready to gang up with men in a single-minded approach to a common goal. Willing to sacrifice self and immediate benefits for long-term gain. Attracted to either exotic or submissive women. Some TWs find rape appealing.	Except in the case of a few dominant lesbians, admires and is sexually attracted to robust and successful masculinity. Yet relates better to recessive men who will not oppose her. Frightens off some men by her attitude but faces the dilemma that she cannot respect a man who fails to stand up to her. Regards domestic work as drudgery. Demanding in terms of acceptable holidays. Very ambitious for her children.

Male True Professional	Female True Professional
Interested in developing personal skills on a long-term basis. Likes mentally demanding work or technically complex craft work. A collector, connoisseur or expert in one or more particular fields. Capable of working alone but adjusts well in intimate relationships with one or two chosen friends or work associates. Not comfortable as a member of large groups or occupying a place in a hierarchy. Ready to share or swap duties with wife or partner if a suitable arrangement can be reached by negotiation. Sophisticated in musical tastes and/or reading.	Sees her long-term goals in terms of professional fulfilment. Likes mentally demanding or creative artistic work. Takes little more than an incidental interest in domestic matters. Keen to ensure she can resume her career if interrupted. In seeking a mate looks for partnership and companionship. Happier to establish a relationship with someone in a professional field that differs from her own. Negotiates her way through situations making competing demands on her time but finds it difficult to fully reconcile working and family life. Sophisticated in musical tastes and/or reading.

Male True Slave	Female True Slave
Physically well-built, hard-working and loyal. Responds well to clarity and firm authority. More comfortable when undertaking 'tasks' than in discharging responsibilities. Prefers practical to mental work. Enjoys leisure activities that involve physical expression, such as dance and energetic sports that involve training and application. Relies on mother figures for support and decision-making guidance. Unpredictable in marital relationships.	Works hard to oversee family. Ready to become the breadwinner in households lacking a male. Shows respect for people and institutions. Supports religion in the community and will offer her services for unpaid work on its behalf. Liable to be exploited by males but often will return exploitation and unrequited love with unselfish service. Does not bear a grudge when she is imposed upon. Sexually compliant.

The likelihood that individuals will exemplify one of the prime archetypes in all manifestations is limited due to the complex ramifications of inheritance. Hybrid characteristics are likely to be more frequently encountered. Genetic hybrids in the botanical field generate a range of outcomes extending from the most useful to the least useful characteristics of each parent. However, in the case of humans these genetic behavioural pulls can be modified to facilitate their operation in a desired direction. Below I have set out on the left hand side the most favourable outcome (i.e. most problem-free) and on the right hand side the outcome likely to prove the least favourable (i.e. most problem-prone).

Hybrid Male Primaeval Warrior	
Favourable	Unfavourable
Strives to make his mark as a business or political leader, but can also thrive as a supervisor or controller in a structured organization. Shows leadership in dealing with groups. Capable of self-sacrifice on behalf of his in-group. Protective towards those he seeks to lead. Values his family life but prefers to keep to the 'male' role in domestic relationships. Best adapted to the type of woman who likes to serve him and fill the traditional female role.	A reactive approach to the demands of a job. Makes a poor subordinate. Inclined to be domineering. Prefers to spend his leisure time in all-male company and/or in outdoor sports. Attracted to expeditions offering excitement and challenge. Takes women for granted. Ready to exploit them for personal pleasure.

Hybrid Female Primaeval Warrior	
Favourable	Unfavourable
Ambitious for her family and keen to progress in terms of personal interests but less where this involves personal employment. Believes in gender differences and that it is a 'man's duty to keep a wife'. Likes a man to be a man but has firm views on how men should behave. Ready to entertain her husband or partner's clients and friends but likes to be firmly in control on the domestic front. Runs a well-kept household. Operates best in home territory where she feels in full control over her environment.	Where she enters employment, most likely to become the 'dragon in the office' without necessarily proving more effective in getting others to do what she wants. Fights for female rights and will take a leadership role in all-female groups. If thwarted at work glad to give up a job to give her more freedom and to 'run her own show'. Bold and sexually self-confident with men but feels more comfortable with a submissive male partner if one can be found.

Hybrid Male Primaeval Professional	
Favourable	Unfavourable
Finds fulfilment in typical male occupational roles such as engineering and or makes his mark as a manual craftsman. Likes to design or use tools. Should his occupation fail to provide the outlet for his interests, likely to become keen on DIY. Expects his partner to complement his activities with traditional female skills. Likes to travel as part of his working life or if that is not available likes to explore unfamiliar areas or to camp. Resistant to taking holidays organized by others. Generally contented with his way of life.	Treats occupation as if a personal hobby. Should that not prove fulfilling, puts leisure interests before the call of the job. Develops personal skills and ready to contribute these, where appropriate and appreciated, but resistant to relate these to a wider set of needs. Opposes the entry of women into men's traditional field of work. Unwilling to help in the household unless the task fits the 'male' image.

Hybrid Female Primaeval Professional	
Favourable	Unfavourable
Aspires to run a home and her profession simultaneously. Employs labour where the opportunity allows and can manage domestic staff with skill and discretion. Strives to keeps her personal and professional activities separate but can handle them both in a balanced way. Takes an interest in husband's or partner's work without interfering. Intent on establishing an integrated life-style. Will sacrifice job and career opportunities should these conflict with the demands of home life.	Develops female skills in artistic areas that have no employment or domestic advantages except in the context of entertaining friends. Spends leisure time in pursuit of very personal interests, for example in reading fiction, to neglect of her family. Finds herself torn between meeting husband's or partner's demands and pursuing her own interests. May succeed in creating her own philosophy of life but then finds it does not always fit in with the preferred life-style and expectations of others.

Hybrid Male Primaeval Slave	
Favourable	Unfavourable
Ready to engage in any duties or physical work that comes his way but does so more readily when he perceives these as generated by the demands of the community. Feels comfortable when working in or for an institution. Creates self-imposed work in order to improve the home. Engages in hunting or fishing mainly 'for the pot'. Reluctant to trespass into 'female' territory. Holds firm views as to what constitutes male and female work. But otherwise makes an appreciative and dependable spouse.	Dependent on others to provide work and direction. Inclined to work hard at things that have become outdated. 'Retreats' from life when the pressures become too great by finding alternative pursuits that make a heavy demand on personal time. Often needs a male role model in order to motivate and to find a route back into the mainstream of economic life. Steady and reliable in a marital relationship. But dependency on a mother figure or on a wife makes him vulnerable to general decline if his props should disappear.

Hybrid Female Primaeval Slave	
Favourable	Unfavourable
Reluctant to venture far beyond the home or immediate community. Makes a good domestic servant or service worker. Capable of combining duties at home and work but sees the role of a woman to put family first. Shows courage and endurance in putting up with misfortune coping whatever the prevailing circumstances. Acts in the belief that Fate has decided. Given to superstition but entertains no set of consistent beliefs. Hopes that men will supply what is missing in her life but is reconciled to the fact that they don't always come up to expectations. An uncomplaining survivor.	Actuated by an internally directed and reactive feminine life-style. Lives a parochial life to which she will settle down quite comfortably and uncomplainingly. But if that becomes disrupted, turns into a typical fatalist who accepts 'come what may'. Easily exploited by men on account of naivety. Reluctant to say 'No'. More likely than other women to be 'employed' in a brothel, and to be resigned to its life. Finds difficulty in escaping from an unacceptable way of life. Needs a strong figure on whom to lean.

Hybrid Male Warrior Professional	
Favourable	Unfavourable
Nurtures high ambitions and exudes drive. Shows initiative from an early age and finds ways of using any acquired skill to commercial advantage. If all goes well, drawn to work in a company that is a global player. Content to travel extensively if the job calls for it. If frustrated in plans or ambitions, keen to create his own business. Should it fail, possess the resilience to start again. Expects his wife or partner to fit in with his life-style. Needs to be boss if he is to work well with others.	Too impatient to make a good student and opts for short cuts to meet his goals. A self-starter who displays talent but one who finds it difficult to work with colleagues. Capable of achieving success and then spoiling it through lack of social intelligence. More difficult to live with than other types of professional worker but will settle down well with an 'admiring' wife.

Hybrid Female Warrior Professional	
Favourable	Unfavourable
Ambitious and a self-starter. Wants to compete with men on equal terms in a given vocational area. Leads from the front. Denies gender differences as being significant. Quick to note violations of 'equal opportunities'. Acts as the standard-bearer on behalf of women. Believes that men can be reformed and improved once women assert their rights. Displays personal ability and likes to work with people whose talents she can respect. May have difficulty in finding a suitable man to whom she can relate in her personal life. Likely to eventually choose a partner who is 'submissive'.	Defies conventional pressures and prone to quarrel with her next of kin. Does not see why women should take on all the domestic roles. An aggressive attitude to men but benefits from sufficient self-belief and a readiness 'to do her own thing'. Capable of starting and running her own business. If no other option is available, the female most likely to become self-employed in the 'world's oldest profession'.

Hybrid Male Warrior Slave	
Favourable	Unfavourable
Dedicated to achieving some personal ambition. Not easily deflected by set-backs. Will work hard to produce results and confront whatever opposition is encountered. Leads by personal example but finds it difficult to delegate work to others. Could flourish as a self-employed worker, who takes the long road to success, given the support of an indulgent wife. But more likely to find fulfilment in a structured organization, which places high demands upon him yet expects him to accept responsibility.	Leads an active physical and sexual life. Resistant to education. Respects strength and authority. Has difficulty in relating to those of equal status. Continually assessing relationships in terms of who is the more dominant. Prone to bully those less well placed competitively. Engages in violent behaviour if frustrated or bored. Loyal to male gang members. Has difficulty in establishing stable relationships with women. Settles down best when presented with charismatic leadership and demanding physical challenges.

Hybrid Female Warrior Slave	
Favourable	Unfavourable
Strives hard in respect of anything she undertakes. Will use personal initiative wherever she thinks it appropriate. Personally undertakes any work if she thinks it has not been done satisfactorily. Will stand up to those she thinks stand in the way of progress but at other times will show herself compliant and responsive where she takes a favourable view of the situation. Can be quite successful, occupationally or in a marital context, where these two aspects are managed strategically.	A legatee of one of the main genetic consequences of the Age of Conquest. Often difficult for her to establish a true sense of personal identity. Genetic history inclined to repeat itself. A high level of endurance towards physical and sexual abuse. Complies with demands and capable of generosity towards those she trusts. If frustrated prone to turn aggressive. Erratic in behaviour and attitude. More prepared than other types of women to exploit her sexuality in a political way for personal gain.

Hybrid Male Professional Slave	
Favourable	Unfavourable
The capacity to work tirelessly towards an end goal without the encouragement of promising intermediate results. A knowledgeable and dedicated student of his subject. Avoids friction and creates few problems for colleagues or bosses. A stable employee and model worker in his field. Takes his married life for granted and unlikely to participate in extra-marital affairs.	Focuses on a particular skill or goal to the extent of becoming stuck in a rut. Subject to 'tunnel vision'. Treats leisure life as a distraction. Somewhat insensitive in relation to his choice of co-worker or marriage partner. Inclined to let personal matters take second place. Lacks the initiative to redesign his life in the event of job loss or marriage setback.

Hybrid Female Professional Slave	
Favourable	Unfavourable
Dutiful in home and at work. Studious in planning and preparation. A self-starter in furthering her education and/or improving her qualifications. Strives to keep in place her domestic world while also being ready to innovate in her own professional field. Would claim to put home first in the event of conflict of duties. Yet colleagues would still rate her more dependable than most.	A hard-working person who avoids the limelight. Inclined to take on more than she can manage. In consequence others may suffer the fall-out before she has time to notice and respond. Equally, maybe prone to the effects of personal stress through trying to take on too much. Results not always commensurate with the effort she puts into things. Persists in managing her domestic and personal life on a particular pattern even when the signs suggest it is time for change.

for reasons of time and space that I have not extended my analysis into these three areas.

Genetic diversity in a complex society creates a range of problems. One of the most pressing of these is crime. Crime is often supposed to relate to poverty but as the wealth of society has risen there has been no sign that crime has fallen. If anything, crime levels have risen. In unsophisticated, low-income and socially homogeneous societies the incidence of crime is often very low. Aboriginal communities can seldom cite anything more than incidents of dispute, which are settled between families and within the community. Even at the present day with rising material affluence there are islands with small communities, such as Tristan da Cunha and Iceland, where there is little or no crime and where prison comprises little more than a cell in a police station. So the question must be raised: to what extent is crime a part of the genetic legacy?

I believe an answer can be ventured at least in respect of our four prime genetic types. The nearest we can get to True Primaevals is to take account of contemporary aboriginals who live either in remote locations or on the fringes of urban communities. Here the record of these two groups is quite different, for only the latter seems to constitute a problem. Apart from drunken behaviour, their principal crime is pilfering. Here the values of a 'caring and sharing' society need to be taken into account. Property scarcely figures as a central concept, since the people, the land and all that it yields belong to Mother Earth. Pilfering is therefore like 'gathering'. In a hunter–gatherer society this is not much of a crime and, notably, the commonest female crime in urban societies happens to be shoplifting. Shoplifting may be reckoned the surest symptom of a True Primaeval. So there are grounds for supposing that there are more True Primaeval Women around than there are True Primaeval Men. Here there is a contrast with True Warrior Men. The prison population is well stocked with those who have committed crimes of assault, robbery, rape and malicious damage. Overwhelmingly these are male rather than female crimes, from which one might deduce that there are far more True Warrior Men around than True Warrior Women. True Warriors constitute other menaces that do not always conflict with the law. As befits their origins, they try to start wars, or engage in aggressive litigation, in the name of the group for which they present themselves as saviours. True Warriors can appear as 'great patriots' and many would prefer to act in accordance with the law, if it can be so represented, rather than openly violate it.

Now consider the crimes that might be associated with True Professionals. The first observation to be noted is that the prison population contains very few blue-collar inmates with craft or trade skills. Crimes of True Professionals are more frequent among mainly white-collar workers, typically involving fraud, forgery and embezzlement, sometimes linked with computer crime, which also includes computer hacking and the deliberate spreading of computer viruses. Here there are signs that 'seeing what they can get away with' is part of the motivation for the crime. True Professionals like to act 'professionally' when they find themselves in situations with tempting options. The very low incidence of crime among True Professional Women may suggest the rarity of the true type and reflect their slow emergence in evolutionary terms from their genetic roots.

Finally one has to consider True Slaves. Strangely, or so it may seem, I am inclined to believe that this encompasses one of the smallest groups of criminals. Procreating Slaves, unlike other slaves, were selected for their personal qualities as well as for their robustness. Those personal qualities were founded on respect for person and property. Slaves who stole might be killed or suffer the direst penalties and only the honest were entrusted to become procreators. By historical progression slaves turned into serfs and in due course into peasants and small-holders. Their incomes might be low but their response was to work hard as their forebears had always done. Many criminals react in the opposite way. They look for the lazy, short cuts to success. As for women, True Slave Women possessed qualities of hard work and devotion, often making fine nurses. Unfortunately True Slaves were also available for sexual exploitation by True Warriors. The resulting progeny produced a hybrid group of Warrior Slaves, possessing a genetic inheritance that was seemingly capable of pulling them in opposite directions. Yet their attributes could also be combined to yield a particular blend of aggressiveness and compliance. Such a mix provides the ideal genetic foundation for the criminal gang. That risk is heightened whenever Warrior Slaves are domiciled in particular areas where their concentration gives rise to a Warrior Slave culture.

Many of these problems may be difficult to tackle but understanding their nature provides leads. Warrior boys can be trained in vigorous team sports before they become Warrior Men. They can be taught the sportsmanship that goes with the tradition of each game. Respect for opposing players can be cultivated with a corresponding respect for women. Cultured behaviour needs to be revived. There are many conventions that are now slipping into disuse, like 'never swear in front of a woman' and 'opening doors' on their behalf, sometimes ridiculed as condescending or sexist. Socially engendered respect for women is the best long-term guarantee against rape.

In the case of women prone to compulsive shoplifting one suspects a root cause lies in the frustrations of True Primaevals. The need to 'gather' and to 'make for the home' has been taken away from Primaeval Women by the march of 'progress'.

Academic ambition has been foisted on to some, for whom it is unwelcome, and in so doing ousting traditional feminine arts, crafts, skills and pursuits. Domestic Science is treated as a lower grade activity and is beginning to disappear from some classrooms. An educational system that was more responsive to the genetic orientation of its students might do much to develop and stabilize personal identity. With reference to True Professionals, the prospects are improving for reducing the crimes to which they are susceptible with the growth of Business and Professional Ethics as core elements in vocational education. Professionalism is an honoured word. Those who work within its frontiers are being urged to uphold its best traditions. And finally to help True Slaves, more needs to be done to enhance the dignity of labour and reverse the notion that mental work is intrinsically superior to work that is physical.

All these considerations suggest that populations should be seen less in gross terms as clones of some given culture. Rather they can be viewed as individuals wrestling to find a true identity and often struggling to find a place between cultural pull on the one hand and their genetic roots on the other. There is an equal need to understand both the genetic forces disturbing peaceful communities and the way in which commercial and cultural pressures are running counter to our genetic inheritance. Only when such forces are fully appreciated can the necessary steps be taken to restore balance and harmony in society.

11

Gender relationships

I have argued that since *Homo sapiens* became a new and established species on the face of this earth, evolution has continued its relentless passage in a way that has been seldom noticed. Whereas evolution had once focused on modified anatomical forms to facilitate behavioural change, during the Age of Power psychogenetic changes took place, as a result of natural selection, without any physical changes being visibly evident. While people tend to be conscious of ethnic differences, the differences that have most far-reaching effects on human behaviour relate to the four basic groupings human evolution has left as its legacy. The four pure forms comprise Primaevals, Warriors, Professionals and Slaves. All four have interbred so that the human scene has been bequeathed a minority of true types and a multiplicity of hybrids. Such diversity has greatly complicated gender relationships.

At this point it is worth restating what has taken place during the evolutionary period covered by this book, for what reasons and with what result. The starting-point is the primaeval human community, whose members followed the biorhythms of nature. They looked for food when they needed it and the reward for sufficiency was leisure. Men and women needed each other in forming a balanced community. Its essence is embodied in the yin–yang theory, which originated even before the first Chinese empire was established in 221 B.C. That age-old philosophy rested on a belief that perfect harmony lay in the balance of opposites – darkness and light, summer and winter, passivity and activity. The pairing of the yin and yang corresponded with the roles of female and male respectively and was held to reflect the make-up of Nature. That philosophy might be explained as expressing a psychogenetic tendency that had a biological basis. Men were not disposed to do the sort of things that women did and women were not attracted towards the activities in which men engaged; they preferred complementary rather than competing relationships. So life-fulfilling was that pattern of living in its purest form that their direct descendants (surviving aborigines) have been treated as 'unemployable'. In effect they will not fit in with the demands of a well-structured 'nine-to-five' job and will go 'walk-about' rather than sacrifice a life-style in balance with Nature.

That essentially free way of life largely disappeared for most of humanity once population pressures or natural disasters, or both acting in combination, finally dislodged primaeval men and women from Paradise. The needs of survival then called for a variety of adaptations in response to changed conditions and unfamiliar territories. These skills and adaptations were based on the development of what had existed beforehand. Gender relationships were affected but only marginally in terms of their basic nature. Women who made clothing from skins now succeeded in fabricating clothing designed to offer protection from the most demanding climates. Whereas women had identified and gathered plants that could be served as nutritious food, they now began to select plants as crops that could be planted locally and harvested. Men who had developed tools for purposes of hunting now refined those tools to serve a wider range of purposes, producing new designs and new ways of manufacturing products. These patterns continued in a rudimentary form throughout the Great Migration.

But when the great tide of migration had completed its course and all the easily habitable land was divided up, a new era opened up for our species. The Age of Power arrived and with

THE STORY OF HUMAN EVOLUTION
Illustrating alternating periods of equilibrium and sudden change

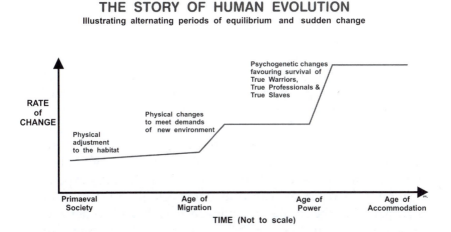

TIME (Not to scale)

it gender relationships were to be transformed for thousands of years. Grafted on to the basic models of male and female humanity new specialized varieties of humans came into being as the outgrowth of the unremitting pressures of natural selection. So the genetic legacy added to its portfolio – True Warriors, True Slaves and True Professionals. The relationship between men and women now became confounded by this new set of human variables.

But to what extent have the underlying basics changed? The prototypes of the human species live on as archetypes, often modified by cross-fertilization, but still reflecting the shape of the society for which they were once perfectly attuned. The problem under modern conditions is that hunter–gatherers can no longer live as they did before. Archetypal Man can no longer go hunting, either singly or with a male group, in order to kill and bring home fresh produce for the household. Yet he is still expected to 'bring home the bacon', that is by taking on his role as the 'breadwinner'. And if he can no longer fulfil his economic and domestic function through hunting, he can at least gain some personal satisfaction by taking up fishing as a sport or paying to shoot pheasants or paying extravagant sums to shoot stags or big game in Africa. But that diversion operates at the expense of gender relationships. Archetypal Woman, for her part, can no longer go foraging in the wild for plants or fruit with which to feed the family. Much less is now to be gained by sowing crops for the purpose of subsistence or in applying her natural skills for making use of whatever materials she can lay her hands on in order to produce clothes or other objects for use in the household. Much of her practical ingenuity has been rendered obsolete by the availability of cheap goods in the supermarket. To redress the balance she can cultivate the garden to grow flowers and culinary herbs with which use to apply her skills and interest in cooking, and she can decorate the household with whatever she can purchase and keep the home in good order. Should she drive her car to the supermarket, she will treat it as a 'gathering' expedition, delighting in what she can find unexpectedly. And back in her own neighbourhood she can engage herself with other women in voluntary activities on behalf of the local community or religious organizations. Occupationally she can find a role in running a local crèche for infants where her social aspirations will be met by her contacts with other women. Such activities are overlaid on the exercise of her domestic skills in running the home. Yet here her sense of fulfilment is limited to the extent that her work has been de-skilled by modern technology. Greater freedom in the use of time is being counter-balanced by loss of fulfilment at home.

Yet other aspects of the male–female relationship may remain undiminished in so far as men and women deal with their respective domains. Our True Primaeval housewife will demand of her returning husband that he take off his outdoor shoes and put on his slippers and mow the lawn and cut the hedge, while she herself prefers to attend to those parts of the garden that require specialist skill and knowledge. Her husband may appear a dominant figure in *his* own domain, but he will still defer and readily comply within *her* domain. A gender adjustment is needed when the pair leaves the house and goes out in the car. Now Primaeval Man will take the steering wheel, for our bonded pair has now entered the 'remote' (male) domain. His partner, while quite capable of driving to the supermarket, will now decline to do so, preferring to pass on the leading role to the male. That is how patterns of activity and role allocation appropriate to Primaeval Men and Women have been transposed in modern society. The very continuity in the pattern of such relationships over a great span of time attests to the strength of the basic model.

True Primaevals are important for understanding our species because they were prototypes of 'natural pairings'. Once pair-bonded, they were made to match. The behaviour to which one individual was prone corresponded with the other's needs and expectations. Mutual dependence makes for enduring comfort so long as it can be separated from vulnerability. Primaeval society was able to cover that vulnerability because the community was ready to render support for gender relationships with a range of traditional practices and customs. True Primaevals favour a balanced life-style in tune with nature. Unfortunately for them, this ideal often conflicts with the demands of the modern world. Those who pursue what they consider a balanced life-style contribute less to the gross domestic product and lack the status of those who are fully active in the economy. But once retirement beckons, the pressures are lifted. A new ethos is accepted and True Primaevals become fully adjusted to the life that unfolds.

Whatever problems True Primaevals face in gender relationships in the modern world, these are far surpassed in the gender relationships of True Warriors. For the latter, the issue is competition and in a domestic contest there can only be one winner. One person will need to give way and for True Warriors that is difficult. But there is a solution. While for True Primaevals the separation of territories is organic, for True Warriors respective territories can and need to be staked out. The front garden can be treated as the property of one partner, the back garden another. Decisions on handling and paying bills, on purchases for the household, on schooling for the children and on the length and nature of vacations can be parcelled out as being the responsibility of one or the other partner rather than be treated as matters necessitating mutual agreement. That is the best case scenario. In the worst case scenario, no agreement is reached. But there is still an overriding problem that relates solely to Warrior Man, now displaced from the Age of Power and recast in the Age of Accommodation. Warrior Man and his fellows who dominated their epoch still need to *prove* themselves as warriors. Ideally, Warrior Men need another group to fight and, when they have won, they are genetically programmed to claim their reward by raping the women found in the conquered territory. But such a natural disposition, implanted by Evolution, comes up against the frustration of contemporary circumstance. In modern society both assault and rape are illegal. The best hope of substitution for some males lies in joining an all-male football crowd for an away match where they can invade another's territory. There will be every chance of a fight with the opposing side's football supporters. And given the fact that football supporters belong to a large 'army', effective police intervention is seldom adequate to prevent the battle. When victory is won, or sensed as being won, the supporters will drink heavily to celebrate the joyous achievement. But now where are the spoils of victory? Where are the women? There are none available to rape, for the law has excluded that possibility. A lesser option for the invaders is to consort with prostitutes, who can now become the imagined victims of the defeated side. When that alternative is ruled out, Warrior Men will sublimate by singing bawdy songs or telling bawdy jokes about women. Then Warrior Man on returning home from the victor's orgy will be prone to violent behaviour towards his submissive woman.

This then is the archetypal pattern within modern society for the Warrior Men together with their preferred womenfolk who are the legatees of the Age of Power. It is a pattern devoid of the stability characterizing the relationship between Primaeval Man and Woman. But there is an additional complication for our Warrior pair. Whereas Primaeval Women behave in a predictable way, Warriors' women do not. Although selected in the first place for their submissiveness, the aggressive streak of the Warrior is liable to be bequeathed to the daughters of the Warrior so that they may take after their fathers rather than their mothers. Their real nature may emerge as that of True Warrior Women and equal in belligerency to the menfolk. In the past such attributes of behaviour would be restrained. In a truly patriarchal culture submissive female behaviour would be enforced by the *paterfamilias*. But in a largely cosmopolitan world the culture is different. In the new scenario some Warrior Women have emerged uninhibited, ready to flaunt themselves in their true colours, and are not to be trifled with. And because their sisters who physically resemble them may be truly submissive, Warrior Men are confused about what they can expect from women in general.

Now consider the third of our archetypal groups, the True Professionals. These are the descendants of those whom the

Conqueror selected and the Ruler protected on account of their superior trade skills. The trades themselves have been rendered obsolete by the march of technical progress. The spread of literacy has made commonplace that which was once rare. But the descendants of this special elite are still around, now embracing another image and enjoying an elevated status. Their common feature is that they act as though they have a mission – their prime vocation is to fulfil themselves in those fields for which they have an aptitude. Professional Woman, unlike her Primaeval counterpart, does not centre her interests on the household. She does not accept the gender roles and stereotypes that others consider appropriate. She expects her husband to take a due share in those general duties that underlie their basic existence. In the ideal scenario, archetypal Professional Men and Women are flexible and often inter-changeable in their domestic roles to the extent that duties and responsibilities are decided in a flexible way by mutual agreement. To that extent they are a viable pairing, well suited to survive the pressures of modern life. But patterns of behaviour often fall short of the ideal scenario. The devotion of Professional Man to his profession and Professional Woman to her profession sets the scene for a *parallel* rather than a *complementary* way of life. The more active the duo in their separate professions, the greater the chance of a conflict in priorities.

In a world becoming ever more complicated, other issues are growing in topical urgency. What happens when Warrior Man pairs up unknowingly with Professional Woman? What can one expect when Primaeval Man pairs with either Professional or Warrior Woman? The result is likely to be a misalignment in gender expectations. Both parties face the prospect of disillusionment. It is more difficult to predict what may happen when atavistic features of behaviour occur in various permutations. But again, there are sharp contrasts between attractive and unattractive scenarios. Consider the case of a woman whose professional and primaeval nature is in equal balance. She may succeed in managing them in tandem, focusing on her professional career but being house-proud at the same time so that as a Primaeval Professional she may manage to extract the best from these different strands of her genetic inheritance. If she were to extract the worst of these strands, she would

What modern Warrior Man demands from Professional Woman: 'Where's my meal?'

What Primaeval Woman asks of Professional Man: 'What have you brought me home today?'

display disinterest in domestic life and a casual approach to her occupation as impinging on her leisure life. Such a pattern would make for very unstable gender relationships.

Another specific set of difficulties arises when two different genetic roots combine in a hybrid form. Often Warrior Professional Woman runs into difficulties in intimate relations with men, especially in connection with her opposite number, a Warrior Professional Man. Comparable problems arise for a Primaeval Warrior Man. He is prone to difficulty in cultivating stable relationships with the opposite sex, for on the one hand he will expect a gender-based division of labour (from primaeval make-up), while on the other hand he is prone to be aggressive and interfering in her domain (from his warrior nature). Each of these hybrid personalities needs to come to terms with the issues they face. There are some limited strategic options they can pursue should they seek to manage themselves to better effect (see Table).

In all matters of gender relationships much may depend on the genetic behavioural profile of the prospective partner. Here appearance offers no sure guide. A smartly dressed, cleanly shaven man may be truly primaeval in his basic behaviour, while a person of informal appearance may act in all respects like the classic Professional Man. It is not merely personal features that may mislead but also the style of dress. The latter is determined by the norms of the cultural setting which favour a particular fashion. Convention makes it likely that this uniform will be heeded irrespective of the true nature of the person who wears it. A True Primaeval will not disport a loincloth but may be wearing a formal city suit.

Behavioural cues rather than visual ones also offer the only sure leads in the case of True Slaves. But then, in the perception of many, the visual has tended to override the behavioural and for understandable reasons has placed an emphasis on ethnic characteristics. That is because Africa was once the warehouse for the world supply of slaves to the Americas and the Arab world. In consequence, slaves were expected to be Black because history produced that result. In reality, Africa contains True Warriors and a smaller supply of True Professionals but, unlike slaves, few have been exported to other continents. Contrast Africa with India. India has exported segments of its population to many parts of the world but seldom in the context of slaves. Indians who have emigrated have been largely drawn from the moneyed and business classes. Many fall into the category of being True Professionals with superior abilities. Their descendants have prospered even as minorities in host countries. While True Slaves may include many Blacks, varying according to the region of the world, it is not of course colour of the skin that determines whether or not a person is, in psychogenetic terms, a True Slave. In Europe nearly all True Slaves are White. That is because the general population is White. There, the genetic legacy from slavery has been extended in time and genetically diluted. The reason is slavery died out in Europe long before it died out in Africa. The descendants of slaves in Europe passed through the intervening and prolonged period of serfdom before they merged into the general population. True Slaves possess common characteristics irrespective of geography and colour of skin (embracing Blacks, Browns, Whites or Yellows). That is because True Slaves were highly selected for procreation by slave-masters in terms of their *personal qualities* – capacity for hard work, endurance, respect and personal loyalty. These qualities have given them considerable advantages over True Primaevals in employment, especially in the growing field of personal services. But True Slaves are at a disadvantage in comparison with True Primaevals in some other respects. The delicate balance in gender relationships between men and women was never a factor in the formula for the evolution of the archetype. True Slaves were thrown together for procreational purposes virtually at random and never had enough freedom to evolve into a real community. Hence True Slaves, unless unified by authority or religion, are prone to lack a sense of common purpose. As a consequence, True Male and Female Slaves, in the absence of some unifying code of beliefs, may experience difficulty in keeping their marriages intact.

Yet in this field there is one factor that needs to be borne in mind. Not all former slaves should be classified True Slaves (as I have defined it), since many were originally snatched from primaeval communities, where community spirit and a balanced life-style including the pursuit of leisure were the order of the day. It was their very innocence and lack of defence capabilities that made them victims for slave-traders. Such circumstances generated a large body of Primaeval Slaves. From such hybrid roots slave cultures have emerged and have taken on a vigorous identity. The culture of the Primaeval Slave is very evident in the Southern States of the USA, giving rise to some of the most significant music and singing of the twentieth century, while also doing much to transform the nature and outward forms of traditional religion.

Yet in other ways the Age of Power has continued to cast its long shadow over slaves and their descendants. That historical legacy emanated from the total power exercised by slave-masters over the women they fancied. In the era of slavery rape was a capital offence if committed by a Black on a White. But it was no offence at all, in its more usual form, as an action by a White on a Black – with inevitable results. So it came to pass within the community of slaves and their descendants a minority of Warrior Slaves emerged and eventually moved out of their original communities in search of 'conquest' in big cities. There they have come to exert their power in shanty towns. Strong, aggressive and dangerous, they have proved difficult to keep within the bounds of the law and the most prone to engage in marital violence. The turmoil of the Age of Power thus gave rise to a set of behaviours that were genetically programmed to continue from one generation to the next, although often operating in irregular steps. The complexities of the interactions between our four main archetypes have certainly made it difficult to predict the long-term outcome in relationships between mutually attracted couples in the modern world. It is important however that people should be aware of the range of possibilities that can exist.

These archetypal issues are not the only problems that need to be faced in the Age of Accommodation. There is a deeper biological problem that may have roots in the Age of Power and is psycho-sexual in nature. Studies in Sexology by Terman, Kinsey, Masters and Johnson and others have brought to the fore the diversity of sexual behaviour of women, features of which are liable to become out of balance in respect of the sexual behaviour of men. It has been estimated that approximately fifteen per cent of women are unable to achieve sexual orgasm irrespective of their experience or of the character of their partner. At the other end of the psycho-sexual scale an estimated fourteen per cent of women have a capacity for multiple orgasms exceeding that which can be easily met by any *single* partner. Such a capacity equips a minority of women for the 'world's oldest profession' but jeopardizes the main-tenance of stable gender relationships. Maladaptive psycho-sexual behaviour is a feature of a minority of men just as much as is of women. Women who are unescorted at night or even those who walk alone in the country are liable to assault and rape by men and, less frequently, to be murdered after the event. Such incidents may be isolated but are by no means rare. Some men are evidently motivated to rape and rapists are known to include married men. So how has this maladaptive behaviour originated? And could both forms of maladaptive behaviour be connected?

Earlier in this book I have emphasized the interconnection of events in the story of human evolution. Ultimately the search for territory appropriate for population needs led to warfare between peoples. The standard pattern was that the victors would then kill all the men and all the women, or would kill all the men and spare some of the women. This is why there were surplus women in ancient society, swelling the ranks of second wives, concubines and harlots. Women were raped whether they were killed or not. It is clear why warriors became rapists. But it is not so clear which women were spared. I have argued that women with normal sexual patterns and stable relationships are more likely to resist rape ('a fate worse than death') and are therefore more likely to be killed. Surviving women would be more likely to be asexual (it would not affect them as much) or hyper-sexual (enabling them to cope). It is not a hypothesis that can be verified. But I prefer it to the alternative and more commonly quoted explanation that female orgasm has not properly evolved and is therefore irregular in its distribution, for there appears to be no sign of such anomalies in aboriginal society. I look upon the Age of Power as being the primary source of distortion of basic male–female relationships. Whatever the preferred explanation, psy-cho-sexual anomalies are one further problem to complicate gender relationships in the contemporary world.

While I have taken up the focus of psychobiology to account for patterns of behaviour between men and women, one cannot ignore culture in this context. The passing of the Age of Power and the advent of the Age of Accommodation has brought with it a shift in values. In my next chapter I will focus on where this continuing shift is likely to lead. But for the moment it is sufficient to examine where the current shift has reached and what impact it is likely to have on gender relationships.

A radical new vista has opened up which sounds truly positive. Its name is 'Equal Opportunities'. Equal Opportunities is seemingly the opposite of Subjugation, just as Subjugation was seemingly the opposite of Partnership. Do two apparent opposites, expressed as ideals, bring one back to the same starting-point? Does it imply that women have regained what they lost in the primaeval era? It cannot be so, since the original gender partnership was based on a natural division of labour. The term 'Equal Opportunities' embodies an ideal. Its

'So that's settled then. You do the dishwasher, the front garden, service the car and make supper on Friday and after a year we reassess.'

significance is that it brings in its wake 'Equal Expectations' of access to the *same* jobs. In other words, men and women are now in *open* competition for jobs, for roles in society and for roles on the domestic front. There are no social guidelines that are generally agreed. There is no sense of gender partnership. It is the end of the yin–yang philosophy. Freed from domestic chores by labour-saving devices, women are now entering the labour force in unprecedented numbers. Given the breakdown of former social structures, it does not seem surprising that marriages are dissolving at a record rate and that research has shown that marriages are dissolving faster in countries where women have their highest economic participation rates. Are marriage breakdowns the price that has to be paid for emancipation? Or can something be done to retrieve the position?

There are grounds for supposing that women have not evolved genetically as fast as men in the last ten thousand years. The heavy involvement of men in wars has given rise to higher differential survival rates, operating against True Primaevals and in favour of True Warriors, True Professionals and True Slaves. Cross-gender transmission will have passed on some of these genetic characteristics to women. But apart from these cases, the forces of natural selection will have acted less energetically on the psychogenetic characteristics of women. The overall effect is to make it likely that True Primaevals will be found in larger numbers among women than among men.

Even so, average patterns will have no bearing on individual cases. If relationships in marriage are to withstand the economic pressures of modern life, more people will need to anticipate the possible options and contingencies that lie ahead. This means posing the 'what if?' factor. There is value in couples discussing their outlook on life, including its many twists and turns, before they proceed into an intended lifelong relationship. Understandably, there is often a reluctance to do so. Mutual attraction takes over and masks underlying realities. Values, priorities in life and general outlook do not readily surface in courting couples. Even family background can deceive. While knowledge of family history offers leads, the genetic route through the Ages takes so many paths that its history can hardly be traced in terms of known and meaningful determinants. It is more important that people make their own discoveries about each other freed from any preconceptions.

The four basic archetypes created by human evolution offer a framework for starting the process and a guide as to what the future can promise. The various permutations that spring from these archetypes, modified by stray symptoms that do not always 'belong', help to make individuals what they are – individual. A more sophisticated world has made the conduct of individual relationships more difficult. But by gaining a better understanding of how individuals are made up (in terms of their archetypal construction) such problems have a better chance of being overcome.

12

A changing culture

Culture has an enormous capacity to absorb those who fall into its bosom. This appetite to digest and mould all it consumes means that a strong culture can eradicate individual differences, at least at the superficial level. The larger the culture or institution, the more standardized its demands, the more total its capacity to assimilate. Large groups are conservative in outlook and follow traditional norms. But suppose the group is penetrated by a few who are distinctly different in some particular feature. At first nothing may happen because a few individuals may be insignificant in relation to the mass. But once the few come together to form a coherent body, the situation changes. Small teams have a character of their own and are disposed to create their own norms. Sizeable minorities even have the potential to effect change in larger groups, for mathematically they alter the ratio between conservatives and innovators.

Now suppose a group of babies were exchanged between millennia so that each cohort formed a sizeable minority in a larger group. Those who take the line of this book, which is that human nature has not stood still, would expect to see some dramatic effects. Hunters who do not wish to remain hunters would disturb an aboriginal culture, especially if they were genetically programmed to behave as True Warriors. Similarly, True Professionals would have difficulty in adapting to such a culture. The mix would not work. All that may be idle supposition. So invert the question and consider what might happen were True Primaevals to be uprooted at an early age and raised in the modern world. The answer is now not a matter for speculation. This is the type of transposition that has already happened and the observation is that the expected level of cultural assimilation has failed to take place. That position applies in the case of pure-bred aborigines in Australia. Northern Australia contains one of the largest (uncontaminated) aboriginal populations in the world. The attempt to educate and employ them in the ways the Western world imposed has all but been abandoned in favour of leaving their cultures relatively undisturbed. There is, it seems, one factor in relation to culture that has been largely overlooked, which is the genetic make-up of the population. A homogeneous genetic make-up of the population will make for a homogeneous culture. Cultures cannot be expected to shift very far when their genetic basis remains fixed. In the past, new cultures have arisen because the genetic make-up of the population changed as a result of natural selection or cross-breeding. Large culture changes evidently took place during the Age of Power when the necessary pre-conditions were met. The Age of Power *bred out* those personal attributes of character and behaviour that belonged to the Age of Respect and lacked competitive advantage in the struggle for territory. In their place the Age of Power *bred in* aggressive and destructive qualities round which cultures were built. However, what was useful throughout the Age of Power has now lost its value for the survival of our species and indeed now threatens it. If that is accepted, there is a case for arguing that the evolutionary path pursued for thousands of years would benefit by being put into reverse, at least in a number of key areas. But is that likely to happen?

The first glimmer of hope arises from the fact that the Age of Respect, in which women achieved a position of status, influence and recognition, is not actually dead. The genetic basis may be smaller but is still there. Potentially the Age of Respect could rise again, given a change in circumstances and a recovery in woman's place in society. In considering the chasm that has to be overcome, it is as well to consider how far culture has moved away from the yin and towards the yang. The Age of Power has witnessed a massive cultural shift away from small intimate societies, in which women thrived, towards another form of culture based on large groups run by a male hierarchy with its accompanying bureaucracy. Women have had difficulty in coming to terms with that change and have been ill at ease with its demands ever since. A symptom of this cultural change is that in the contemporary world the larger the group, the smaller is the presence of women at the helm or in any significant position. This point is well exemplified by a millennium summit of world leaders, which was held in the year 2000 at the headquarters of the United Nations in New York. Only ten women leaders were numbered among national governments in the world. Of these, a mere three women leaders attended out of more than 150 leaders present at the meeting, while the remaining seven preferred to send male representatives! Women tend to opt out of what may seem to them male-type armies.

There is now increasing evidence that men and women *collectively* behave in very different ways. Men gravitate towards large competitive groups and vie with each other for positions in which authority can be exerted. Women prefer closer, more intimate and personal associations. As the Age of Power recedes and gives way to the Age of Accommodation the world is moving away from a culture that is wholly masculine in character. A new shape is coming into being which owes much to the continuing emancipation of women. They are assuming a new significance as a political and managerial force as a result of their growing penetration into the wider economy and a rise in their personal incomes. Information technology has opened its welcoming doors to those whose special interests lie in communication and have the added advantage of nimble-fingered keyboard skills. As the old brawn-based industries decline and new lighter industries emerge, a shift in the gender balance of employment is moving many women into key positions. Inevitably such a shift will bring about permanent cultural change. The question to be posed is: what can we expect to be the principal shift?

While there can be no certainty, one eventual outcome is probable. The most likely is that society will move away from organizational forms that have warrior characteristics. In their place organization will revert to the primaeval, with smaller and more intimate features. Such a move, rather than being backward, will constitute a forward step. It will be sophisticated primaeval, in the sense that it will bring with it the intimacy of teams and a devotion to community. And it will also be sophisticated in the sense that, in a world of high technology, communication is more efficiently served by lateral information flow and local decision-making. It is this combination which will appeal to women and eventually gain their support. But its impetus does not come solely from being gender-related. There are other radical forces pushing in the same direction. Small groups and teams, which technology brings into existence are by their nature resistant to Power and to Power-seekers. In so far as the movement towards 'small is beautiful' gathers pace, the Age of Power will look increasingly obsolescent. People will conspire together to clip the wings of potential Rulers and industrial tycoons. Power is not trusted and nothing in its record suggests that much can be gained by putting the clock back. But there are positive lessons to be learned from rediscovering the more remote Past, taking account of what is of value and discarding those features that kept our remote ancestors in a primitive state. Respect for the community and each other and for Nature offers a model for living that is already evoking an ever-widening response. There will be increasing pressure to replace large groups with small groups that are empowered to act on their own initiative and that enjoy wider terms of reference. Events are already moving in that direction. The larger the country, the greater the pressure towards secession on the part of provinces and former states. In the public sector, the emphasis is shifting from large hospitals to primary health care in local areas. In the private sector, small and medium enterprises are outstripping unwieldy conglomerates in the number of new jobs and the range of new ventures they create.

All these trends towards smaller organizing movements are drawing the world closer to the more intimate primaeval communities from which we originally sprang. As such a movement gathers pace, women are likely to figure. They are likely to appear at the forefront of smaller, more intimate, bodies. Their focus will be on improving communication, on seeking to find consensus, on utilizing the talents of those they hold in high esteem instead of trying to compete with them. They are more likely to oppose large prestige projects and redirect priorities to meeting local community needs. For family reasons working women will wish to spend some time at home. They will be less attracted than men to the appeal of creating and inhabiting large, 'power-centred', headquarters and they will show increasing aversion to long-distance commuting which centralized bodies bring about. Hence they will show growing favour towards the dispersion of industry and commerce and specialized professional services.

As Power recedes, the lid of repression against women is being lifted. Women have developed aspirations inconceivable a few centuries ago. In response, the doors of opportunity are being opened for them. And yet it does not follow that the main body of women will march through its portals. Their genetic archetype that gave primaeval society its original shape makes it likely that many women will decline to avail themselves of the opportunities being presented in a competitive, unisex, labour market. Primaeval patterns *still* persist in their adapted form in modern society, for many modern women prefer to remain homemakers, to manage the local domain, to manage their husbands when they enter the home. They enjoy selecting and gathering produce and in making things for use or decoration in the household. They find fulfilment in nurturing the family and caring for and supporting relatives, including older people. The roles they take up and their attitudes would find a fitting place in the primaeval community and they have not died out.

And yet a full reversion to primaeval society is very unlikely to come about. The reason is that humans have become so biologically diversified during the evolutionary march. Such diversity reduces the probability that humans in the modern world will produce a homogeneous culture. The 'warrior' element is too strong to allow the primaeval to take over. Modern man is still dominant, competitive and, certainly in his younger years, aggressive. Evolution has promoted these changes and in so doing has opened up a social and ethical distance from woman. But woman has also evolved because some of the genetic changes that affected man during the Age of Power have been passed on to woman. While aggressive and sexually active men are high in testosterone, physiologically, it is now established that women are also found to produce testosterone (in far smaller quantities) to supplement their oestrogen. Where this happens they are more assertive and sexually proactive. Some women now resemble men in their behaviour and overtly more so than at any time in human history. At one time such women would have been suppressed. Now appropriate roles for them are being found.

This cross-gender migration of characteristics equally applies to men. While women were 'selected' over many thousands of years for their submissiveness, that quality has migrated to the male of the species. The sperm count of men has been falling over a wide area and for a long period and it seems some men are losing their 'masculinity', both sexually and in their habits. Small numbers of men have a fetish for dressing like women, even without being homosexual. This blurring of gender distinctions, whatever its cause, underlies a trend in social policies towards a unisex system of social organization.

The consequences of the complex evolutionary process suggest that evolution has had the effect of moving many women out of the former feminine mainstream and into a smaller set of fast-flowing streams that have no confluence. There will be significant numbers who have inherited from their remote male ancestors aptitudes and talents for which men were spared and protected by their conquerors. Such inheritance will give rise to career women who will put careers ahead of family interests and who are less likely to seek or find a stable relationship with a husband or partner. However, there will also be many women who occupy an intermediate position. They will seek to pursue a career but they will also place high store on the needs of their family. These women – products of eras that have pushed in two different evolutionary directions – will look for compromise but will find compromise difficult. Their voices will need to be heard, not least because they may well one day encompass the majority of the female population of developed countries and as such are sure to form a significant political lobby. They are bound to exert an effect on political culture, facilitating feminine emancipation, while protecting the roles and demands of traditional women.

Now a separate question needs to be asked: how far will these radical socio-economic changes impinge on the culture of beliefs, including religious beliefs? The big world religions have perpetuated their doctrines and practices in the face of many forms of *external* pressure and persecution. Yet how far will they withstand *internal* pressure and erosion from within? Women are not only regaining their influence on culture, but they are now entering its inner sanctum of religion, the priesthood. Such an infusion coincides with an extension of knowledge about the Universe on the part of the educated masses. Rockets and satellites and radio telescopes have explored the Heavens. The former home of the gods in the glittering stars has been revealed as a mass of fiery gases. The residence of God in the sky is steadily disappearing from credibility. As women secure their place in the priesthood and wield their rising gender-presence, the religion of the male, the all-knowing, all-embracing, Almighty is on the wane. It persists primarily in those areas of the world where war and conflict re-emphasize the need for a powerful figure and Protector. There the prophets of one Almighty will battle against the prophets of another, drawing on their warriors to wage the struggle against infidels and heretics. But elsewhere, as Peace casts its sunshine over the land, conditions are created for a cultural change. There is less persuasion in the messages of sin, of punishment against those contravening divine judgement and of virtue through mortification of the flesh. In place of that harsh religion, reflecting times of oppression and violence, the old, feminist, religion is being rediscovered. Heaven has come down from its remote celestial location to a more immediate presence on Earth. In a rekindling of animism, Spirit is being rediscovered, is pervasive and embraces the natural world in its totality, uniting people previously divided in the re-emergence of something closer to holism. This transformation has been taking place over such a long period that its existence has been barely perceived. But now that the dust has settled, a new picture is emerging. God is losing His position into which He was installed in the Age of Power as the Almighty. Instead God is re-appearing in more feminine form as the God of Love.

The level of resistance of world religions to feminine penetration depends on the age of the religion. The older the religion, the more impermeable will be its core and controlling mechanisms. The drawbridge can be raised and the dwindling defenders can retreat to the citadel. No 'true' religion will ever fall to assault, however strongly besieged, for each culture attracts its adherents whose archetypal background guarantees its perpetuity.

The wider significance of any erosion of support for the religious establishment lies in its fall-out. A void is created that invites new religions to flourish. A new climate places less emphasis on top-down doctrines and offers more opportunity for social participation in outward expression and in the formulation of core values that bind together its members. New social participation religions are now invading the territories formerly monopolized by religious orthodoxy uniting people in new 'tribes' of belief. Such penetration is, of course, being resisted vigorously in those countries where Religion and the State combine in the interest of mutual self-protection.

New open, social religions are not the only ones disturbing established spiritual culture, for 'private' religions are also multiplying in the form of cults. New cults with their special mysteries have rediscovered the dynamic nature of earlier religions but have done so at the price of insulating themselves from the outside world. In the search for a new pattern of living many cult-members have been exposed to exploitation by racketeers. The most trusting have even been lured by the mentally unstable into mass suicide. What is more noteworthy than the sensational nature of such incidents is the continuing search by so many people for a new paradigm based on intimate association and fellowship. By being bonded together in a common belief they become a community, flourishing beyond the reach of centralized power. It is an exposure of what is currently lacking in an overpopulated and depersonalized world.

Those genetic forces and impulses that are welling up from below have no adequate outlet in modern society cast in a rigid and depersonalized form. And yet modern society urgently awaits reconstruction. There is an evident need to regain the balance and symmetry of the primaeval community. But can such a goal be attained without losing the refinements of civilized living? How far can the harvests belonging to two earlier and widely separated Ages be reconciled in the new Age of Accommodation? That accommodation will only come about through a new form of Leadership and Management, more social in focus, which will facilitate the growth of a new culture – one that allows for the broadest expression of human development.

13

A question of Leadership

Leadership is never more important than when people feel lost. Lost people commonly look for salvation by choosing a True Warrior – one who embodies all the characteristics of a mighty Conqueror. Once such a Leader has gained the authority to lead a large group, there will be no turning-back on the exercise of Power nor any prospect of eventual resignation. The only end to the career of the Warrior-Conqueror is premature death or disaster for the multitude.

The modern world has backed away from accepting that type of Leader. If Power is not to be the basis of Leadership, what alternatives exist? Already absolute Power has been curtailed in modern society by being subjected to legal or constitutional constraints. And yet most organizations are constructed as though absolute Power structures were still in place. The Chief Executive Officer stands at the apex of the organization above lesser Managers who themselves have lower-placed personnel beneath them. Power has been replaced by rank, a form of pecking order, offering systematic control within a hierarchical structure. Any action lower down is the responsibility of someone higher up. Where decisions need to be taken, upwards referral becomes the order of the day. Given the reporting nature of accountability, there is reluctance to delegate responsibility as this implies loss of control. Anyone who relinquishes personal authority may feel vulnerable when faced with the consequences of mistakes and the prospects of blame.

While many hierarchies may appear flourishing and intact, their hold is being steadily eroded by the impact of the new technologies. In the older industries many senior managers had served as man and boy. Knowing the jobs from the bottom up enabled them to make decisions on the basis of their greater depth of experience. Now, in the age of information technology, much innovation is entering the organization from the side and even percolating in and being acted on at lower levels. Are such initiatives to be suppressed as out of line with hierarchy? Or are they to be encouraged? The impact of information technology is to create many new open-ended situations and thereby to provide a different type of opportunity for Leadership.

However, there is not much to be learned from the old system about Leadership because, irrespective of personal qualities, being the Leader was the position to which a person was appointed or which he achieved through power struggles or assassination. Only *after* the position was gained, could those qualities be assessed. Now the situation has changed. When Leadership is discussed, it is usually in a forward-looking context. It is about the *prospective* advantages of moving someone into a leading position; it is about the type of training, education and experience appropriate to the creation of a particular sort of person. Such a person is hoped to have the stature of a visionary change-agent.

It is at this point that a dilemma arises. The problem centres on how Leadership relates to rank. In practice it is difficult to separate the two, for only if the possessor of the desired qualities operates at the appropriate level can such qualities be used to full advantage. Certainly one can contemplate the difficulties arising when a talented person displays Leadership qualities in the presence of a more senior manager. What can one then expect? Certainly embarrassment, possibly friction. One likely outcome is a personnel transfer or an eventual loss to the company of the person whose contribution is judged to 'rock the boat'. It is easy to see that hierarchies equate Leadership with what they consider the characteristics of their own interpretation of Management.

155

The concept of Leadership also faces another testing dilemma. Leadership is prone to draw on biological roots. Someone who takes the lead in a group is likely to be dominant and aggressive, to provoke and to be excited by social challenge and to 'see off' competitors. People will recognize a True Warrior. The True Warrior will lead the tribe to victory. These are the characteristics that have been bequeathed to humans genetically by the Age of Power. Whether the cluster of characteristics found in a True Warrior has any correlation with the talent that a lead role demands is often questionable. Yet the tendency for groups to be submissive and to seek 'Leadership' will usually catapult the claims of the more dominant and less talented over the talented and less dominant.

Now consider the issues of Leadership from another angle. Detach it from personality and rank and consider it instead in relation to *status*. Take the case where there is no such thing as *rank* and people work together in a team and relate to each other from a position of equality. Now what does Leadership mean in this context? In a team of limited size, dominance produces no advantage, for it is quite likely to be counter-productive and resented. Individuals who emerge positively in a team do so because they offer *excellence* in some aspects of its activities, being much appreciated by their peers as valued contributors. But that excellence is not seen as *absolute*. Members of a team are not excellent at everything. If the team is well balanced, excellence is likely to be distributed between several people who will shine in turn as issues revolve round their particular strength.

A person considered excellent by peers gains *status* and respect and from those roots is well placed to provide Leadership. Hierarchical managers in large corporations or even in high tech companies may be unaware of such attributes, for they have no clear figures by means of which status and respect may be measured. Even where teams produce the desired results, the key role played by any one team-member will not be discerned merely by attention to the output. While team-members see their peers in terms of status, members of a hierarchy see them in terms of rank with its marker-posts of salary, car, size of office and other perks. These two differing perceptions produce a divide around the concept of Leadership separating those who view the world from the standpoint of structures and those who favour team-work and networking.

Higher-ranking people are *expected* to take the lead in every situation, even where they lack the knowledge or the skills. Perhaps they do so because they *feel* they are expected to do so. To fail to do so would be to relinquish Power. Such pressures mean that Leadership based on Rank suffers for that reason from a susceptibility to inadequate feedback and so fails to measure up to the common interest. Such Leadership hogs Power and restricts the personal development of potential rivals. Here lies the contrast with Leadership based on Status. The person who is provided with the space in which to lead is licensed to do so *only* because colleagues recognize the aptitude in the person as being appropriate to the situation. Such a person is granted a temporary licence. If the situation changes and the aptitude is judged inappropriate, the licence is withdrawn, whereas Leadership by Rank enjoys a permanent licence.

The two roots of Leadership have political forms. Leadership based on Status provides many of the benefits associated with political democracy, while Leadership based on Rank is subject to the inefficiencies found to beset the Age of Power. Rank often consolidates inefficiency because it cannot be challenged from below, so its inherent limitations have to be countered by other means. Power is tempered in a democratic society by 'checks and balances'. These serve a positive function as they act as the ultimate safeguard against abuses. But they also have their downside. Safeguards of this nature undermine personal respon- sibility and introduce protracted delays. In the resulting morass of uncertainties it is easy to see why people hark back to Leadership based on Rank, where there is always clarity in decision-making.

Finally, a new image of Leadership has come to the fore in the age of mass communication: it is Leadership by Reputation. In the highly populous societies that make up the contemporary world people do not see their Leaders but only *know* about them by a manipulated process. Such knowledge is mediated and embellished by professionals who possess special skills as image builders. The more money invested in their activities, the more effective are the results they can show. Reputations are distorted to allow images to be met. At times of mass crisis, people look for heroes and saviours. That very situation amplifies the image of a potential Leader who now only has to live up to the reputation that Hope and Public Relations have created.

It is a shortcoming of modern democracies in large countries that they revolve round Leadership by Reputation. Democracies purport to offer direct elections by allowing voters a choice between candidates they 'know' only by manipulated Reputation and facial charisma. Only good-looking candidates are likely to be elected. A better choice might be to opt for a broader rather than a centralized mode of Leadership. That would imply the creation of an interacting, multi-cellular, system involving candidates of whom voters had *personal* knowledge. Such a radical step would involve recasting large-scale depersonalized society into smaller-scale personalized operations. People are more likely to make better judgements when they know someone personally than when they *hear* about a candidate. In effect therefore there is an important organizational choice to be made on the coming political agenda. Is it a better strategy to seek Leadership from Status? Is it better to allow lower levels (i.e. with smaller remits) to find and to project their own *known* Leaders, and for them to enter higher bodies, which in turn adopt the same procedures in a set of escalating steps? This would have the effect of dispersing Leadership through different groups and levels. Or is it better to retain the present system offering a mass ballot for a Leader, who is presented, built up and projected on to the electorate on the basis of Reputation and given strong controlling powers over subsidiary bodies? The choice between these two systems will have an important bearing on what comes to pass in the twenty-first century.

A suitable form of Leadership is certainly essential if the century is to be one of progress. With the benefit of hindsight it is easy to see that the greatest limitation in the Age of Respect was its *absence* of Leadership. That is because the primaeval community revolved around consensus and consensus is essentially conservative in its mode of operation and in its outlook. Innovation took place but only in a reactive context and over a protracted period of time. The Age of Power introduced a form of Leadership that had previously been lacking in human communities. Rank destabilized the old communistic societies and brought in many advances that would otherwise have been unlikely or impossible.

But Leadership by Rank, having served its time, is becoming increasingly out-of-line with the developing needs of the Age of Accommodation. Leaders who are seen as seekers and wielders of Power are vulnerable to those who seek to disparage the over-ambitious and are ready to 'cut down tall poppies'. Both workers and executives respond unfavourably to the introduction of outsiders brought in to 'lead them'. People like to lead but do not like to be led. Now candidates eligible to become Leaders are expected to show modesty and humility when presented with the prospect of high office. The Speaker in the House of Commons in Parliament is dragged to the Chair. A candidate for the Presidency of the United States is more likely to be nominated by conspicuously declining the prospect of High Office until drafted in by popular acclamation. Such a pattern illustrates the large shift in values between those that are now coming to the fore and those that once prevailed during the Age of Power.

There is therefore a lesson to be learned. Successful candidates must first win support from their peers among whom they will need to establish status and win respect. Leadership through Status, acquired by those with intimate knowledge of the person, offers the surest guarantee that Leadership of the *right* type will emerge. Managing without Power is the precondition for discovering latent talent and enabling it to flourish, while also offering the surest guarantee against abuse.

14

Two modes of management

Contemporary society stands at the crossroads between two eras. Now a choice has to be made as to which road to follow. The Age of Power produced a distinctive style in management and government, which depended on a general acceptance of Authority. In that culture authoritarian figures thrived. Underlings who accepted the leaders they were given felt secure and without them they felt lost. When an absolute monarch died, the masses looked expectantly for the next king. In the absence of an undisputed successor, someone had to be imported even if he came from another country and could scarcely speak the indigenous language. Society could not function without a monarch, or so it was believed. In a similar way at the present day many corporations consider they cannot function without a strong Chief Executive. The Age of Power continues, even though weakened, as the outgrowth of a long period of evolution in which aggression and dominance and respect for size was bred into the human psyche. Yet Evolution began to change direction as soon as Power ceased to offer territorial advantages for tribal or national expansion. The competitive advantage of the exercise of Power has waned because new forms of collective security now either punish or at least curb aggressors. It has waned on the social and industrial front because Power, even in its most civilized form, is failing to manage organizations in an adequately efficient, flexible and creative way and in a style that is acceptable to those who are being managed.

Humanity has halted at the crossroads while the signposts are being read and new directions considered. The route to the Age of Accommodation is beckoning. It commends itself because organizations are becoming multi-faceted, both culturally and technically, with a wider range of stakeholders and a multiplicity of objectives. The new route is beckoning because better-educated people seek a degree of personal and collective autonomy which hierarchies cannot offer. It is beckoning because, with the growing proportion of women entering professional and managerial employment, the traditional seniority of men over women is being challenged. The era that is unfolding is calling for new modes of working relationship and new modes of decision-making. That does not mean that the old modes are finished. The needs of the old era and of the new continue to exist side by side. The old order continues because even when Evolution points in a different direction the genetic disposition of people cannot change overnight. Even given an extended period of time, long-existing attitudes that were built in during the Age of Power are likely to persist among a wide section of the population because changing conditions are no longer operating on natural selection. Those who are 'less competitive' are no longer being left to perish, as they were in the past, nor are they being deliberately exterminated by the depredations of war as they were when the Age of Power was at its most ruthless. They are now freed from biological competition. Those who are the least economically active, have lowest incomes, are the least skilled and the most poorly educated have higher rates of reproduction than the rest of the population. The laws of Nature, operating on the evolutionary process over a vast span of time, have seemingly been put into reverse. A far more politically complicated situation now needs to be managed.

Under such circumstances there can be little doubt that two eras will continue to live side by side in an overall framework within which the differences will increasingly sharpen. What is current is to a large extent what has existed in the past. Most senior managers are both genetically and culturally products of the Age of Power. Such managers may be designated P-type

Managers. The best examples of the P-type make their mark for a variety of virtues. With boundless energy and drive they lead from the front. They are fearless decision-makers. The organizations they establish and control benefit from clarity of structure. They accept personal responsibility for everything that falls under their aegis. They look for appointees who show personal allegiance and loyalty, which they recognize and reward. Such P-type Managers are clearly people of talent performing a valuable function, even if the era to which they are best suited is now becoming subject to an ebb tide.

The contrasting A-type Manager is a response to the Age of Accommodation. These managers are more social beings and less sensitive to the threat of competition. They are less keen to establish conspicuous individuality, for they are acting on behalf of the whole. They downplay any temptation to engage in personal domination and prefer to spread responsibility (and any glory) to others. Their focus lies in setting up self-generating processes that do not require external direction and result in a better balance. They seek to establish the best form of decision-making machinery within viable and sustainable systems. They listen to the messages that these systems generate. They work to ensure that key positions are occupied by the best contributors. A-type Managers share responsibility more often than P-type Managers because shared decisions with colleagues of proven ability widen commitment and increase confidence in the merits of the decisions made.

P-type and A-type Managers exhibit contrasting styles. Both naturally gravitate towards areas where their talents can be used to best advantage. P-type Managers thrive wherever their brief incorporates a single overriding objective. There, typical masculine drive and focus are shown to greatest advantage. The best example in the commercial world lies in the need to improve 'the bottom line' on a regular annual basis. Power and resolution are needed to cut out functions that fail to make an unequivocal and unarguable contribution to profit. Typical measures include cutting down on Training, Research and Development or cutting direct labour costs in a number of ways – by restricting or eliminating salary rises or through outsourcing components and materials, often resulting in switching contracts to suppliers in low cost countries. There are other instances where such singlemindedness can yield conspicuous results. The clearest example relates to war. Countries at war take the view that they must win 'at all costs'. That belief helps to ensure victory. The high price that must be paid in other ways is merely set aside. But there are other types of victory outside the military arena and where a prime objective also becomes the focus of effort. Many large companies are managed as though their supreme aim is to become the biggest in their field. Other companies, already big in their own fields, strive to grow beyond their acknowledged areas and become conglomerates. In both cases the prime focus is set on acquisitions with the help of merchant banks. Such ambitions are pursued without regard to the effect on share price (usually adversely affected by acquisitions) and without prior consulta-tion with their key personnel and, universally, without reference to their employees. A genetically based form of personal energy, rooted in the need for Power, is driving organizations in their chosen directions. Those directions may be disputed by some and lauded by others. Whatever view may be reached on the merits of a particular choice of goals, P-Type Managers make their mark as achievers once given the powers they require.

While many P-type Managers are admired for the qualities they possess, increasingly one hears the admission: 'Yes, but he's the wrong sort of manager for this organization'. A-type Managers are seen to correspond more closely with the stated needs of the times and the diagnosed needs of the organization. Yet P-type candidates still retain their competitive position by outshining A-type candidates in recruitment events. There are several basic reasons why this should be so. A P-type Manager will make bold claims about personal achievement (in the past tense) and about what can be achieved (future tense). Focused individuality usually outshines the endeavour to create a better balance or a better team. A-type Managers are scarcely in a position to make convincing claims about what may be achieved in conjunction with others and are unlikely to make the attempt. Given the void in competition for a new mode of Management, P-type Managers in hierarchical organizations are prone to create self-perpetuating cultures, drawing on forces that are deep-rooted in the human mind, fashioned by thousands of years of exposure to the Age of Power. It is often difficult for people to envisage how an organization can continue to function effectively once a commanding figure is removed unless there is a similarly 'strong' replacement.

Yet in spite of these obstacles A-type Managers are already making their mark and are coming to the fore by their own distinctive route. They are more likely to be found when promotion is considered *from within* as distinct from relying on external recruitment. That is because those who have worked for some time within a human system generally recognize the person who truly delivers, who can get the best results from people and shows greatest awareness of what can be accomplished in the foreseeable future. Whether or not that person receives the opportunity for personal development *within the organization* is often the most important factor affecting the ultimate emergence of the A-type Manager. No talented A-type candidate, whose career path has not received the necessary investment, can hope to compete on level terms with an introduced P-type Manager with a record that shows continuous salary progression.

That is why the present era has reached such a critical stage. Will A-type Managers break through and prove themselves? Closely allied to that issue is one that relates to the future of women in the new era. Will they rediscover the primacy of the roles they once fulfilled in primaeval society? Will they play a bigger part in holding the community together and rediscovering its sense of purpose? Will they hold together the firm, enabling it to achieve a better balance in the objectives they set themselves? Will they break through the 'glass ceiling', not so much to usurp men at senior levels but to create a better balance in the direction in which the whole is moving?

If the position of women is in this way interlinked with the potential rise of the A-type Manager, the inevitable question arises: are P-type Managers and A-type Managers gender-related? Are ideal P-type Managers quintessentially masculine? Are ideal A-type Managers quintessentially feminine? There is a further question about the distinction between P- and A-type Managers. How far do P-type Managers correspond with Shapers and A-type Managers with Coordinators (using the language of team roles, as described in my earlier books)? In other words, in taking both queries together, how crucial is the distinction between P- and A-type Managers? Or are these distinctions merely reflections of these two other basic dichotomies?

The outlook of A-type Managers is certainly in line with those personal qualities traditionally associated with women. Yet many

164

women in leading positions do not exhibit those styles of behaviour that might have been expected. A conspicuous example of the discrepancy occurred in the case of Margaret Thatcher. The first woman Prime Minister in the United Kingdom was virtually the classic P-type Manager – hard-driving, determined, fixed in her objectives and mistrustful of those outside her inner circle and of foreigners in particular. As an example of what women could achieve in a man's world, she became the icon of leading female achievers the world over. Tougher and more resolute than her male colleagues she did nothing to enhance the distinctive contribution that women can make in a leadership role. Instead she made her mark by underlining the ability of women to become the *equal* of men. Women with contrasting characteristics, who exhibit classic A-type behaviour, make their mark in a different way. Those I have known have risen to leading positions in hospitals and hospital trusts, so that they are virtually anonymous to the general public. The fact that a manager is a woman does not necessarily denote any given style of approach. I feel it would be wrong therefore to equate P- and A-type approaches to Management with gender distinctions.

There is little doubt that strong Shapers are ideally fitted to become P-type Managers. By personality they are fitted to dominate. Their orientation towards achievement gives them the spur to overcome all objections and resistance. And yet there is a problem in equating the two terms. The difficulty arises from the fact that some of the most outstanding A-type Managers and advocates of the approach have, in my experience, been Shapers. How can one explain such an apparent paradox?

My explanation is that they have changed by conversion. Shapers have a proneness to intolerance but the greatest intolerance they show is towards failure. Intellectually able and socially aware Shapers are often quicker than others to see that top-down management does not yield the hoped-for results in a sophisticated and educated world and they are readier to act accordingly. Shapers are often prime movers in change. The first need therefore is to change themselves. After that they set out to change the culture in which they are embedded. Hence I must dispute any attempt to equate Shapers, who embody a particular form of role relationships, with P-type Management, which incorporates a particular philosophy centred on human organization.

I do think it is easier however for natural Co-ordinators to become true A-type Managers. So also it is easier for women to develop as A-type rather than as P-type Managers, in which direction they are sometimes tempted in the quest for promotion. Should that choice be made, the pressures are likely to build up. Men have difficulty in accepting women in a P-type role, are reluctant to feel subordinate to a woman and may undermine them in that role. In a comparable way many women feel uncomfortable in taking on a P-type style. Assertiveness Training has been introduced as one way of meeting the problem. There is no doubt that women can develop as P-type Managers if suitable conditions prevail. But unless those conditions arise and the need is there, one must question whether this is a desirable path for women to follow. It is an observed fact that many women feel a sense of in-born hesitation when they find themselves in direct competition with men. That hesitation is the product of a sort of atavistic wisdom. There is no need for women to follow this route, for they are equipped with primaeval talents for Managing *without* Power.

Men, in contrast, have evolved as Warriors and in the past they have shown how much can be achieved, albeit at great human cost, by Managing *with* Power. Such an approach can no longer operate in an absolute sense but can be modified to take account of those curtailments that democracy and supra-national government have imposed. Given those modifications, many men are now well furnished with the temperament and the personal resources to *become effective* P-type Managers. There are even possibilities that a P-type Manager, in recognizing the merits of an A-type style, will behave like an A-type Manager if the occasion warrants it. Conversely, a woman who stands as an ideal example of an A-type Manager may have to shift her stance in dealing with a serious breach of discipline by switching to P-type behaviour. There is therefore some flexibility in terms of possible behaviours of which male and female managers are capable.

However, to *assume* that individuals will show this flexibility is another matter. A safer strategy would be to enlist management teams of men and women who individually exhibit the most typical, as well as the best, forms of gender behaviour. Such individuals will grow in personal development as they learn to appreciate the contribution of others. By so doing, their corporate activities will produce a wider range of benefits while reducing

166

the risks that more narrowly conceived achievement brings in its wake. In this transitional era between the Age of Power and the Age of Accommodation both basic styles of management can operate in conjunction with one another. Men and women in mixed gender teams can rediscover the mutuality that was such a feature of primaeval society and develop a new management style in the process (for a further note on this subject, see Appendix III: From Equality to Mutuality Action). For the first time in the history of the human species, the spur to continuous progress has become compatible with true partnership in gender relationships.

'Right, we're set up to decide, so now let's decide.'

If the world is on the threshold of a new era in its approach to human affairs, such a movement will need to be triggered by a new philosophy of belief; or perhaps it is an echo of the past, in line with the Biblical prophecy that 'the meek shall inherit the earth'. Such a philosophy must be based on an interpretation of humanity in the natural world and on its progression from the past, to the present and on to the future. That future will only loom large if it appears brighter than the past and if it offers the prospect of solutions that have not hitherto been found. In such a world women have a greater part to play. That enlargement arises not because they are being offered equality in blurred gender distinctions, but because they are fulfilling themselves in influential roles that have their genetic roots in a primaeval society. Collectively they will make their mark in a way that they may fail to do individually. They will wish to make the prime organizing force the smaller community. They will be alert to pollution of the environment and strive towards its improvement. They will curtail the ambitions of weapon-makers. They will re-order priorities in budgetary expenditures. But in so doing they will discover that a growing number of men are pursuing the same path. Men and women have been created by Evolution to work together, often in their separate ways, to mutual benefit. The need is therefore not to change human nature but to rediscover and develop those latent roots on which its future edifice can be built.

15

A final note on the relationship between genetic archetypes and team roles

Team roles refer to the useful modes of behaviour that individuals adopt in contributing to the effective work of a team. These roles were first set out in *Management Teams: Why They Succeed or Fail* and later in *Team Roles at Work*. Research showed there are nine distinct ways in which individuals can make useful contributions as a member of a team. No one is perfect but a team can be, providing the team is well balanced in composition and its members understand that complementary role-play is valuable. Some individuals are outstanding in one given role, some can manage to be valued contributors in several, while a few seem unable to make their mark in any team role. However, while the various starting-points differ from one individual to another, team roles can be learned. In that way individuals can improve their personal effectiveness and become more sensitive to the role of others.

The table below offers a reminder of the classification and significance of the team roles.

Team roles develop through education and social experience. In contrast genetic archetypes, rather than being learnt, are genetically programmed to appear from time to time irrespective of demands or circumstances. While team roles are purpose-driven,

Team role	Significant contributions	Allowable weakness	Non-allowable weakness
Plant	Creative, imaginative, unorthodox. Solves difficult problems	Preoccupation with ideas and neglect of practical matters	Strong 'ownership' of idea when co-operation with others would yield better results
Resource Investigator	Extrovert, enthusiastic, communicative. Explores opportunities and develops contacts	Loss of enthusiasm once initial excitement has passed	Letting clients down by neglecting to follow-up arrangements
Co-ordinator	Mature, confident. Clarifies goals, promotes decision-making, delegates well	An inclination to be lazy if someone else can be found to do the work	Taking credit for the effort of a team
Shaper	Challenging, dynamic, thrives on pressure. Has the drive and courage to overcome obstacles	A proneness to frustration and irritation	Inability to recover situation with good humour or apology
Monitor Evaluator	Sober, strategic and discerning. Sees all options. Judges accurately	Scepticism with logic	Cynicism without logic
Team Worker	Co-operative, mild, perceptive and diplomatic. Listens, builds, averts friction, calms the waters	Indecision on crucial issues	Avoiding situations that may entail pressure
Implementer	Disciplined, reliable, conservative, efficient. Turns ideas into practical actions	Adherence to the orthodox and proven	Obstructing change
Completer Finisher	Painstaking, conscientious, anxious. Searches out errors and omissions. Delivers on time.	Perfectionism	Obsessional behaviour
Specialist	Single-minded, self-starting, dedicated. Provides knowledge and skills in rare supply	Acquiring knowledge for its own sake	Ignoring factors outside area of competence

genetic archetypes are not. As products of Evolution, they remain as ever-present in everyday life as the physical forms that evolved at an earlier stage, like our hands and our brain, except that they are mainly invisible. Whether their presence is beneficial or damaging depends on the prevailing situation.

The main genetic archetypes can be set out as follows:

- **True Primaevals** are disposed to a natural, balanced and complementary relationship between men and women, they aim at a balanced life and thrive on the living community. But in the modern world they are reluctant to adapt to the regular and demanding disciplines of education and employment.
- **True Warriors** provide the drive and the readiness to sacrifice the present for the future. They are action oriented and stirred by challenges and the need to overcome opposition. But their desire for personal or tribal victory can destroy communal harmony.
- **True Slaves** offer service, loyalty and uncomplaining hard work. But they need to be led, for unless they have structure and a sense of direction, they feel lost and insecure. There are limits on to how far they will accept personal responsibility without incurring stress.
- **True Professionals** possess the aptitudes and creative abilities that underpin all forms of technical progress. But their focus on the development of personal skills for their own sake can detract from how well they serve and fit in with the needs of the community.

Team roles probably had their origins laid in these basic archetypes. While there is no exact equivalence between genetic archetypes and team roles, particular genetic archetypes will predispose individuals to learn certain roles. That is why understanding their origins is so important. The closest associations are as follows.

True Primaevals have a strong focus on personal relationships and on the community. Such an orientation does not necessarily turn them into team players. Anthropologists have noted that aborigines (their nearest equivalent) have a strong sense of 'immediacy'. They are not overly concerned with the future, which is often governed by unknowable forces over which they have no control. To the extent that Primaevals are prone to live in the present, they are not assured of becoming good team players in the business and professional world. I have argued in this book that for evolutionary reasons True Primaevals contain a higher concentration of women than men and, in line with that observation, that 'all-women' teams are inclined to lose their sense of direction. For them, the future is unknowable. True Primaevals have the disposition to flourish in the communication roles of Team Worker, Co-ordinator and Resource Investigator, once these are learned. Here women in terms of their personal development have an advantage over men. However, that advantage is marginal in relation to Resource Investigators, for that role is not only social but implies a readiness to explore. Territorial exploration shifts the emphasis away from the female domain into the male domain. Whatever gender differences exist in genetic archetypes, they do not change the essential nature of the relationship between genetic archetypes and team roles.

True Warriors are comparable to True Primaevals in terms of gender differences in their distribution. But here the gender bias works in the opposite direction. For evolutionary reasons there is a higher concentration of men among True Warriors and a relatively lower concentration of women. Moreover, the Warrior archetype manifests itself in a different form from the way it manifests itself among women. The aggression of the male Warrior is directed against out-groups and against individuals primarily in so far as they are members of a group considered hostile. The female Warrior, on the other hand, is aggressive towards an individual solely for *personal* reasons. A man may attack another because he supports the wrong football team; a woman may display her enmity towards a woman wearing the same dress at a party. Yet Warrior characteristic is not a wholly negative attribute, since it also underlies the drive for 'victory'. In the contemporary world victory has taken on another meaning. It refers not to killing and the seizure of territory but to achieving a goal; it depends on drive and determination. Here Warrior behaviour offers a foundation for the development of the effective Shaper. True Warriors have a secondary function, lying beyond personal resolution, they achieve more where they can organize others in proper 'battle formation'. The True Warrior archetype can therefore lay the foundation for the development of an associated team role – the Implementer. Hence the well-organized warrior, who might have flourished in medieval society, can be modified to become a valued contributor within a demanding project team.

Now consider the genetic archetype of True Slaves. These were at one time highly selected. For the most part, slave men and slave women were separated and exploited in quite different ways. To be allowed to breed and to form a continuing community, slaves needed to distinguish themselves in their functions in the eyes of the slave-owners; they needed to accept structure in the way they worked and to prove reliable in accomplishing what they were given. Through the process of natural selection True Slaves came to possess the genetic endowment to equip them to become Team Workers and Completers. But again, such team roles need to be learned. Team Workers need to learn the social and political skills that befit a particular culture. As potential Completers they need to learn the basic trades necessary to achieve the standard of perfection that is required.

True Professionals are well equipped to become Plants and Monitor Evaluators. Their genetic endowment gives them satisfaction from using and developing their mental abilities and a good general education is the only pre-requisite. True Professionals are also well set up to become Specialists given the provision of vocational education and/or training. True Professionals also have some affinity for work as Implementers but here the pre-requisite is practical experience.

On an overview of genetic archetypes there is a human shortfall in the supply of potential Resource Investigators. It is not surprising then that in the story of human civilization, and after the Age of Migration came to an end, many communities became excessively inward-looking and perished. In contrast, trading nations, adequately equipped with Resource Investigators, have prospered. A population drawn to the exploration of new territories will have a particular character. Perhaps that is part of the explanation of why the United States has become the 'Land of Free Enterprise'.

Archetypal distinctions

Team roles develop out of genetic archetypes but they do not obliterate the archetype itself. The archetype can burst through the canopy of culture, given the appropriate stimulus, and so produce 'unexpected' behaviour. It is the 'unexpected' that gives the clue to the archetype. The significance of the 'unexpected' is that where it functions at variance with known team roles or cultural norms, learned behaviour is liable to produce a certain internal strain. That is to say, learned behaviour will be performed with some degree of ease up to a certain level but after that threshold is reached, something snaps. Continuation of that behaviour is then sensed as being 'unnatural'. That is where a sudden change of behaviour takes place, causing surprise even on the part of those who were hitherto intimates of the observed.

Examples are frequently found for each of the genetic archetypes. Consider the case of a professionally well qualified woman, who in reality is a True Primaeval. Her professional standing may have come about as a consequence of her abilities and the ambitions of her family and school to 'push' her. Achievement feeds further ambition. If she is a musical instrumentalist, she will be expected to perform or teach. But a True Primaeval may wish to do neither. As soon as marriage prospects loom, she opts to give up a promising career and choose a life-style that in her estimation offers a better balance.

Sometimes the genetic archetype will burst through to create a crisis. I once knew a talented academic who also combined intellectual ability with technical skill, charm and urbanity. With these qualities he was an asset to the prestigious college at which he lectured. Unfortunately, he was apt to engage in hot disputes with colleagues at meetings over matters that any bystander might view as trivial. In ancient times one True Warrior might well have drawn his sword to strike the other. But in contemporary society the True Warrior is more likely to explode in wrath and walk away. That is exactly what happened. In retrospect, it emerged that the True Warrior had earlier made a successful mark in the Territorial Army where one fancies True Warrior attributes may be highly esteemed. But in a college environment such unexplained behaviour could not be tolerated and his contract came to an end.

True Slaves are also subject to unexpected behaviour, the more so where the positive value of what they can contribute has been greatly appreciated. One has known individuals who have carried out their work with such distinction that they have been promoted on merit to a senior position. They will have accepted their promotion with more reluctance than would have been expected. It is only later that they are found to experience stress in undertaking their new responsibilities. At the first opportunity they are only too glad to accept early retirement.

Many structured jobs in large organizations restrict True Professionals in the exercise of their talents and offer little scope. When that happens, True Professionals tend to look for satisfaction outside their place of employment, developing expertise in hobbies, like painting or model building, even if these have no particular application or commercial advantage. To illustrate, one local government official in her private life was a talented and highly productive graphic artist. But instead of exhibiting her work she hoarded the many items, which remained, for the most part, unseen in folders and her skills went largely unrecognized.

Much behaviour that is rooted in genetic archetypes serves no evident purpose and yet that does not stop it 'bursting out'. Those who are in the business of managing people need to take such phenomena into account. If genetic archetypes comprise the atavistic foundations on which sophisticated societies have been built, we cannot afford to ignore them if projected plans for the future are to be soundly based. Indeed, if it can be done, the future must be built to safely house Primaevals, Warriors, Slaves and Professionals, for each group has the right to exist within a balanced global culture.

Commentary on cartoon themes

'If you bring me back an antelope haunch and a honeycomb, I'll mend your bearskin and have a nice meal waiting.' (page 15)

The greater physical strength and the weapons they choose to carry give men the potential to dominate and subjugate women should they choose to exercise their power. How then was it that in primaeval society women enjoyed high status, respect, influence and relative freedom? While the working domains of men and women were separate and mutually exclusive, pair-bonding provided a continuing and close male–female link, enabling women to use their pyscho-sexual and greater communication skills to communal advantage.

'Sorry tree-spirit. I'll give you a couple of minutes to get out.' (page 29)

Primaeval men and women had respect for each other and for nature. All living beings had spirits, including the flora and fauna of the habitat. The dead, including and especially their ancestors, were in a sense still alive. But all the dead needed to be respected. The spirits of the dead, if ill-treated, could come back to haunt those who displayed lack of respect.

'If you think we're coming on board that on the next voyage, you're mistaken.' (page 44)

The sea-people were more advanced than the fisher-folk both in the design of ships and in navigation. Ships belonged in men's domain and it was taboo for women to enter them, which meant that the taboo had to be overcome if a population was to cross a wide stretch of water. Successful migration would present great opportunities. But maritime travel also involved huge risks. For women to be included they needed to be reassured and finally convinced.

'It looks as though this place is already occupied.' (page 47)

To avoid competing for territory early man put down conspicuous territorial markers in the form of megaliths, monuments and temples. Territorial conflict did not begin until all desirable sites were occupied.

'Just off for four years. Meanwhile no locksmith is permitted entry to the castle.' (page 59)

Warriors needed to go to war and that meant leaving women behind. Such women might be available to lovers unless drastic action was taken. The chastity-belt, various forms of mutilation and incarceration of women all presented options. The loss of sexual opportunity at home was then counter-balanced for men by the opportunities for rape abroad.

'Stop making and growing and do something useful. There's a city waiting to be raided over there.' (page 67)

Construction takes time, skill and effort. Much less effort is involved in reaping the benefits of what others have constructed. So, during the Age of Power, the balance of advantage switched from trade to raid.

'I think this new religion looks promising.' (page 83)

Primaeval society thrived on local religion, local spirits and local gods. This became unacceptable to Empire where an absolute Ruler could only tolerate one form of allegiance. For a time there was a period of uncertainty with major gods and minor gods co-existing. Then order was restored when the religious and secular were combined under the aegis of a single god-king. But during a period of instability, and due to the influence of radical prophets, the two concepts eventually separated. God and the Ruler were recognized as distinct. But all was not lost. Rulers adopted the new religion and helped to transform it into the familiar model of subservience to an Almighty and to a highly centralized doctrine.

'Scribes, coppersmiths and stonemasons fall out. The rest through yonder door.' (page 84)

Conquerors eventually discovered that little was to be gained by killing all defeated enemies indiscriminately. Some were found to possess skills that their own population lacked. Skilled people were sifted out, transported to the home base and set up in ghettos, where they enjoyed special protection for work in serving the Conqueror.

'Ill-treat a prisoner in private? You should do it in public, you fool.' (page 89)

During the Age of Power atrocities were made as conspicuous as possible. If populations were to be cowed by Conquerors and Rulers, all doubts had to be removed about the consequences of resistance or rebellion.

'This has been our third good delivery. So I say: how about electing Nauticus a citizen?' (page 95)

Contact between different people has always presented the option of 'raid or trade?' During the era of the Great Migration, the choice was overwhelmingly trade. The most successful communities were free traders with liberal cultures. They attracted talent and benefited from immigration.

'So what's this you've brought home?' 'It's a book.' (page 106)

Throughout the Age of Power men held all the key positions and women lost virtually all the influence they once enjoyed in primaeval society. They remained totally subservient to men until one technological development totally changed their prospects. The invention of mass-production printing brought books into the home. That medium unlocked a key strength that had its origins in primaeval society – the aptitude for communication. Women took to the printed word and learned from it. Books opened the road to education and emancipation.

'The price of a good slave is getting outrageous.' (page 112)

The ruthlessness of the slave trade produced many evils. But the highly selective nature of the slave-owners' choices ultimately led to a stock of slaves with moral and employable qualities that stood them in good stead well after the termination of slavery. Good slaves were in short supply. With rising auction prices the demand rose for procreating slaves.

What modern Warrior Man demands from Professional Woman: 'Where's my meal?' (page 138)

The genetic roots of humans are never completely covered up and are capable of transcending culture. Irrespective of any common cultural background Warrior Man and Professional Woman will have different expectations of each other.

What Primaeval Woman asks of Professional Man: 'What have you brought me home today?' (page 138)

Primaeval woman expects her man to bring her something home from the hunt. Instead his case only contains the office papers. Neither party can understand the genetic archetype of the other.

'So that's settled then. You do the dishwasher, the front garden, service the car and make the supper on Friday and after a year we reassess.' (page 143)

Before creating a pair-bond, individuals need to examine their genetic archetype and agree on their marital division of roles. Usually this happens later than it should.

'Right, we're set up to decide, so now let's decide.' (page 167)

The decline in 'brawn' jobs and the growth in 'communication' jobs have shifted the balance of economic and social opportunities away from men and towards women. Men thrive in large, power-centred groups (that once enabled them to win territory under the command of a big leader.) Such groups are predominantly all-male but have properties that now make them obsolete. Women prefer small, intimate, mixed teams, where they can fulfil themselves in 'mutuality'. In contemporary society, these are the more efficient. So there is a new direction in which future social organization is likely to move forward.

Portraits of the prime genetic archetypes

Portrait of a True Primaeval

The most direct way of gaining an understanding of True Primaevals is through the testimony of anthropologists. Many of these have expert knowledge of only a single tribe and are reluctant to offer an overview. That is why the more widely ranging *Golden Bough* of Sir James Frazer has special value even though it was written a century ago. The more recent *Cambridge Encyclopedia of Hunters and Gatherers* (1999) is a compendium which contains detailed studies but also one or two general chapters giving an overview of hunter–gatherer society.

An irony of modern life is that, in spite of spectacular increases in material abundance and centuries of technological progress, hunter–gatherers, people who have lived with almost no material possessions, have enjoyed life in many ways as satisfying and rewarding as lives led in the industrial North. Many hunter–gatherer societies have been affluent in the sense of having everything they needed...They spent their leisure time eating, drinking, playing, and socializing – in short, doing the very things associated with affluence. Many hunter–gatherer societies have also enjoyed a great amount of personal freedom. Among the Kung, and the Hadza of Tanzania, for example, there were either no leaders at all, or temporary leaders whose authority was severely constrained. These societies had no social classes and arguably no discrimination based on gender. Their ways of living and ways of collective decision-making allowed them to survive and thrive for tens of thousands of years in equilibrium with their environment, without destroying the resources upon which their economies were based.

The more we learn about hunter–gatherers, the more we realize that the cultural beliefs surrounding modern market capitalism do not reflect universal 'human nature'. Assumptions about human behavior that members of market societies believe to be universal, that humans are naturally competitive and acquisitive, and that social stratification is natural, do not apply to many hunter–gatherer peoples.

The author proceeds to comment on communal decision-making and its advantages:

Market outcomes are based on decisions made by individuals isolated from the rest of society. What is good for an isolated individual in an impersonal market may not be the best for society as a whole. In terms of the social or biological value of ecosystems, for example, it makes little sense for society as a whole to discount them as an individual acting alone would, that is, to claim that they are worth less in the future. From society's point of view it makes little sense to assume that the value of breathable air, drinkable water, or a stable climate continually and sharply declines as we go further into the future. Market decisions reflect the interests of individual humans, not necessarily the community, and certainly not the well-being of the rest of the natural world. We make very different choices as individuals than we do as members of families, communities, or nations, or even as world citizens . . . Here again, there is much to learn from indigenous people. The institution of private property is not the only mechanism to promote efficient resource use. In fact, there is evidence that common property regimes may be more effective in managing resources such as fisheries, even in contemporary capitalist economies, than policies based on the sanctity of individual property rights.

The author finishes with the following reminder of what can be learned from primaeval society:

The modern age is increasingly characterized by despair. Modern society seems out of control and on the brink of numerous irretrievable disasters. The interrelated issues of global climate change, biodiversity loss, overpopulation, and social unrest threaten the very existence of the industrialized North, so seemingly superior to cultures with simpler technologies . . . It is somewhat comforting to realize that the blueprint for survival is contained within our cultural history. Judging from historical accounts of hunter–gatherers, for most of the time humans have been on the planet we have lived in relative harmony with the natural world and with each other. Our minds and cultures evolved under these conditions. Understanding how hunter–gatherer societies solved basic economic problems, while living within environmental constraints and with a maximum of human freedom, may give us a key to ensuring the long-term survival of our species.

John Gowdy, 'Hunter–gatherers and the mythology of the market', in *The Cambridge Encyclopedia of Hunters and Gatherers* (eds R. B. Lee and R. Daly), Cambridge University Press, 1999, pp. 391–398.

Portrait of a True Warrior

Adolf Hitler's imprisonment as a violent revolutionary gave him the opportunity to recount his experiences in *Mein Kampf* and to expound his philosophy. It was the philosophy of one who was still smarting from the defeat of Germany in the Great War; who believed that the situation could be retrieved not by conciliation but by confrontation. He looked to the young for the energy and was convinced that he was uniquely chosen to lead the fight. So great was that conviction that others soon rallied to his call.

At the very beginning of our big meetings, I began the organization of a house guard in the form of a monitor service, which as a matter of principle included only young fellows. These were in part comrades whom I knew from military service; others were newly won party comrades who from the very outset were instructed and trained in the viewpoint that terror can only be broken by terror; that on this earth success has always gone to the courageous, determined man; that we are fighting for a mighty idea, so great and noble that it well deserves to be guarded and protected with the last drop of blood. They were imbued with the doctrine that, as long as reason was silent and violence had the last word, the best weapon of defence lay in attack; and that our monitor troop must be preceded by the reputation of not being a debating club, but a combat group determined to go to any length . . .And how these lads did fight! Like a swarm of hornets they swooped down on the disturbers of our meetings, without regard for their superior power, no matter how great it might be, without regard for wounds and bloody victims, filled entirely with the one great thought of creating a free path for the holy mission of our movement.

Adolf Hitler, *Mein Kampf*, Hutchinson & Co Ltd, 1939, pp. 446–447.

Portrait of a True Slave

Slaves were once commonly looked down upon as virtually subhuman; lying and thieving and fully deserving the treatment they got. That is why so many perished when their immediate usefulness came to an end. But some slaves stood out as the exceptions, possessing such qualities that their lives and lineage were no longer threatened. Harriet Beecher Stowe from her observations as a contemporary relayed that message to posterity. In her famed book, Tom is the slave. When Tom's master died, Tom was sold to another, who in this case was Legree, an evident 'baddie'.

"So ho!" said Legree to himself, "he thinks so, does he? How I hate these cursed Methodist hymns! Here, you nigger," said he, coming suddenly out upon Tom, and raising his riding-whip, "how dare you be gettin' up this yer row, when you ought to be in bed? Shut yer old black gash, and get along in with you!" "Yes, Mas'r," said Tom, with ready cheerfulness

... Legree was provoked beyond measure by Tom's evident happiness; and riding up to him, belabored him over his head and shoulders. "There, you dog," he said, "see if you'll feel so comfortable, after that!"

The author elsewhere gives an account of Tom's relationships with his fellows:

Tom's whole soul overflowed with compassion and sympathy for the poor wretches by whom he was surrounded. To him it seemed as if his life-sorrows were now over, and as if, out of that strange treasury of peace and joy, with which he had been endowed from above, he longed to pour out something for the relief of their woes. It is true, opportunities were scanty; but, on the way to the fields, and back again, and during the hours of labor, chances fell in his way of extending a helping-hand to the weary, the disheartened and discouraged. The poor, worn-down, brutalized creatures, at first, could scarce comprehend this; but, when it was continued week after week, and month after month, it began to awaken long-silent chords in their benumbed hearts. Gradually and imperceptibly the strange, silent, patient man, who was ready to bear every one's burden, and sought help from none,—who stood aside for all, and came last, and took least, yet was foremost to share his little all with any who needed,—the man who, in cold nights, would give up his tattered blanket to add to the comfort of some woman who shivered with sickness,—and who filled the baskets of the weaker ones in the field, at the terrible risk of coming short in his own measure,—and who, though pursued with unrelenting cruelty by their common tyrant, never joined in uttering a word of reviling or cursing,—this man, at last, began to have a strange power over them; and, when the more pressing season was past, and they were allowed again their Sundays for their own use, many would gather together to hear from him of Jesus.

Finally the author, who is clearly focusing on a particular sample of slaves, makes this general observation:

It is the statement of missionaries, that; of all races of the earth, none have received the Gospel with such eager docility as the African. The principle of reliance and unquestioning faith, which is its foundation, is more a native element in this race than any other; and it has often been found among them, that a stray seed of truth, borne on some breeze of accident into hearts the most ignorant, has sprung up into fruit, whose abundance has shamed that of higher and more skilful culture.

Harriet Beecher Stowe, *Uncle Tom's Cabin or, Life Among the Lowly* (1852), Penguin Books, 1981, pp. 557–559.

Portrait of a True Professional

Ideally one would wish to quote entirely from the published writings of a True Professional in order to convey the nature of the person. But True Professionals are loath to write at length about themselves, and prefer to focus entirely on the subjects to which they are dedicated. Hence one is obliged to rely to some extent on what intimate observers have recorded about them.

The person I have chosen as the icon of a True Professional is the late Joseph Needham. Needham read Biochemistry in Cambridge University, later becoming the Reader in Biochemistry and, near the end of his life, Master of the Cambridge College Gonville and Caius. What is remarkable about him is that during the course of his working life he became an acknowledged world authority on Chinese Science, publishing *Science and Civilization in China* in seven volumes in addition to twenty-six other books and countless other scientific papers.

I first encountered Needham in my first year at Cambridge when I was studying Greek, Latin and Ancient History. While students attended lectures in their own Faculties, they were also permitted to attend open lectures. The best attended in the largest University lecture hall was given by Bertrand Russell on the History of Western Philosophy: students occupied all the seats and even sat in the aisles. The least attended was a series of lectures by Needham on Chinese Science and Civilization. So few attended that the venue of the lectures changed, with his surviving students transferring to his personal residence in Chaucer Road. Needham was a somewhat shy man but with a brilliant grasp of his subject which he pursued with intellectual fervour.

How his interest developed in this field is revealed in *Explorations in the History of Science and Technology*, a Compendium complied by his Chinese and Western colleagues to honour his eightieth birthday. Needham once had occasion to lecture on the history of science. He knew that Western science and technology owed a certain debt to Chinese invention but felt he did not know enough about the subject, so he decided to learn Chinese. As a working scientist not far short of forty, this presented him with certain problems. He began by spending a couple of hours each week with the Professor of Chinese at Cambridge. Then he decided that he needed to develop his own method of learning Chinese. Lu Gwei-Djen recollects it as follows:

Needham first visited China in 1942 and on landing at Kunming was reported as being able to converse in Chinese fairly well. As the representative of the Royal Society he was commissioned by the British Government to give some lectures and to 'keep the Chinese scientists in good heart during those difficult days'. Needham was able to travel to many parts of China that were unoccupied by the Japanese in his open-air Sunbeam, flying both the Chinese and British flags on his car. His travels enabled him to meet people in all walks of life and to become well acquainted with Premier Chou En-Lai and other leading personalities. Needham had the unique distinction of being both a Fellow of the Royal Society and an Overseas Member of the Chinese Academy of Sciences.

Lu finishes his essay on Needham with the following:

Meanwhile, Joseph Needham invented his own ways of learning the Chinese language, filling up various notebooks in the process. One thing he did was to set apart a page for each consonantal termination, such as -ien or -iang, with four columns, each for a tone in the national pronunciation, and then on the left a succession of consonantal initials, such as ch-, ch'-, f-, j- and so on. In this way he set up a series of matrix tables, with the meanings of the monosyllable inserted in columns. This helped a great deal the memorization of the words. Another thing he undertook was the making of a dictionary on a new principle, which divided all the characters

188

into four main classes, with a small addendum for 'miscellaneous'. The four were: strokes that went straight down, strokes that veered off to the right, strokes that swerved to the left, and finally enclosures (like k'ou and hui). One could then subsume all the classical 214 radicals of the lexicographers, with all their derivatives, under one or other of these four major divisions. Finally he devoted a large alphabetical address-book to entries concerning those patterns which some Westerners have supposed Chinese not to possess at all, namely the configurations known as grammar. So here he pored over word-order, classifiers, 'empty' particles, numerals, conjunctions, etc. All this was intended entirely for his own benefit, to help his remarkable memory.

How, one might ask, does Joseph Needham think of himself? The answer is revealed in a letter he wrote to Lu Gwie-Dien.

A lifetime in a university environment naturally induces one to weigh up one's own capabilities in comparison with those of others, also scholars and scientists. I have always been very conscious that for sheer intellectual penetration I could never equal many minds that I have been honoured to know – a Waddington in genetics, a Wittgenstein in philosophy, a Woodger in logic or a Fisher in mathematics. What I always sought for was a corner of some field where I could work quietly on, unimpeded by too much company, or too much competition; and perhaps that is the real meaning of 'originality' – chemical embryology was one such field, and the history of science in China was another. The building of bridges is but an aspect of the same thing, because there are not too many people who know both sides of the river, and of the few that do, not everyone feels a pontifical compulsion. If there was any one quality more than any other which made my work possible, I think perhaps it was a queer facility of seeing both the wood and the trees at the same time; in other words the capacity of visualizing broad Sandersonian conceptions, while simultaneously being fascinated by intricate detail, and prepared to do it justice down to the most minute facts.

Here came in an element of the benignly obsessional, for I have always been a picker-up of paper-clips, a collector of rubber bands, signs these of a love of little concrete things, and facts, the building-stones, the 'brass tacks', without which the grandiose generalization will not reveal itself with relative certainty. Careful adherence to precise conventions, helpful filing practices, the management of card-indexes, etc. all proved essential as the large enterprises went on.

At the same time, where possessions other than books were concerned, I have always been conscious of a failure to meet the highest standards of personal life-style, in dress and so on. I could never bother to keep them up, and indeed for years I was much under the spell of the monastic ideal, which reduces possessions to a minimum. Though consciously abjuring the idea of asceticism, there has been something in my make-up which has made it acceptable enough in practice. That was how I lost my father's library, for when after his death in 1920 my mother wanted to dispose of it, I was doubly unworldly, a dedicated young laboratory scientist, and an Oratorian lay brother as well, so I had no interest in doing anything about it, and it was all sold, only a very few books being retained by me as keepsakes. This I have deeply regretted in later years.

Now, today, my greatest wish concerns another library, the one which you and I have built up over the years to serve the project, the East Asian History of Science Library in Cambridge. It ought to serve, not only the project, but generations yet unborn, scholars of all nationalities interested in the comparative history of science who should be free of its treasures, and thus promote a fair and equal world understanding, just as we experienced it in our time. All that it needs now is a permanent building, and all that we need is a chance to see the completion of the project.

Lu Gwie-Djen, 'Needham's first half-life', in *Explorations in the History of Science and Technology in China* (eds L. Guohao, Z. Mengwen and C. Tianqin), Shanghai Chinese Classic Publishing House, 1982, pp. 1–38.

From Equality to Mutuality Action

The Age of Respect depended on a gender-related division of labour and a complementary relationship between men and women. The Age of Power subjugated women and deprived them of nearly all responsible roles in society. The Age of Power also acted against ethnic groups who failed to offer effective military resistance to domination by treating them as inferiors. The Age of Accommodation has attempted to stop and reverse these historical infringements of human rights by instituting programmes of Equal Opportunities and Affirmative Action.

Both these forms of corrective social engineering have produced worthwhile outcomes along with unwanted side-effects. Equal Opportunities as a programme has brought men and women into direct competition with one another, often unsettling inter-personal working relationships and undermining the stability of marriages. The underlying gender problem highlighted in this book is that the basic design of the human community rested on a balance between male and female roles. That balance was destroyed in one way by the Age of Power and threatens to be

GENDER RELATIONSHIPS
IN THE ZIG-ZAG PATH OF CULTURAL EVOLUTION

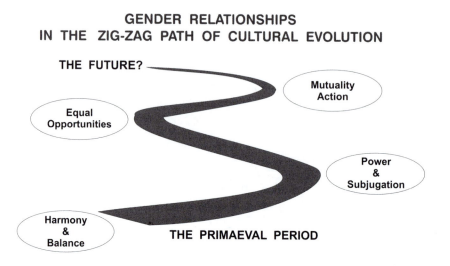

destroyed in another way by the solutions offered in the Age of Accommodation.

Affirmative Action supposes that employment contributions from people of different ethnic origins are potentially the same and that any variation from this pattern is due to unfair discrimination. Where such programmes are put into action, the fallacy is exposed or put into question. If people are appointed other than on merit, the viability of enterprises is put at risk, threatening the security of all employees.

Both these programmes are prone to produce something close to the opposite of what was intended. However, they can be recast to achieve their basic aims by being built around people as they are, rather than around jobs that exist. Here Mutuality Action comes into play.

Mutuality Action has similar aims to those of Equal Opportunities and Affirmative Action but addresses the issues in a different way. In place of an emphasis on the population parameters of the candidates considered for each job, the emphasis shifts to a wider form of treatment. The talents of different groups in search of employment are audited. Those with the most useful range of talents are identified, trained and developed and found appropriate positions. Jobs are built round individuals instead of expecting ready-made candidates to fit into particular jobs.

Differences in treatment between Equal Opportunity and Mutuality Action Programmes, in respect of men and women, are set out in the Table below (see also Chapter 14).

Equal opportunity	Mutuality action
Disregards gender differences in behaviour	Builds on gender differences in behaviour
Promotes competition between men and women	Advocates complementary relationships between men and women
Fosters assertiveness training for women	Promotes team building
At interview questions on family situations are deemed improper	At interview questions on family situations are deemed appropriate
Offers men and women the same working conditions	Recommends tailoring working conditions to meet particular family situations
Treats 'good management practice' as a gender-free concept	Encourages women to develop their own management styles
Assumes there is no basic difference in the work orientation of men and women	Accepts that different working characteristics arise; for example, men tend to be drawn to single long-term goals and women to the more immediate and wider consequences of operational actions
Sees no particular advantage in having mixed gender groups	Believes that mixed gender groups offer a better balance

Background reading

Belbin, R.M. *The Coming Shape of Organization* (Butterworth-Heinemann, 1996)

> Compares human organization with that of the social insects and concludes that there is much that may be usefully learned from the latter.

Diamond, Jared *Guns, Germs and Steel: The Fates of Human Societies* (Norton, 1997)

> A book of remarkable scope in reconstructing world history with an emphasis on environmental rather than genetic factors.

Diamond, Jared *The Rise and Fall of the Third Chimpanzee* (Radius, 1991)

> A zoologist examines what makes us human and provides explanations for much basic human behaviour.

Darlington, C.D. *The Evolution of Man and Society* (Allen & Unwin, 1969)

> A brilliantly erudite and readable account of world history as viewed by one of the leading geneticists of his day.

Frazer, Sir James *The Golden Bough* (reprinted Macmillan, 1990)

First published in 1913 in 13 volumes. A monumental work examining primitive beliefs, superstitions and practices from many parts of the globe. Beautifully written, well conceived and systematically assembled.

Godwin, Jason *Lords of the Horizons: A History of the Ottoman Empire* (Vintage, 1999)

Very readable and informative history of the world's longest running empire. Useful for understanding the Ottoman Empire's unique blend of tyranny and effectiveness.

Hancock, Graham *Footprints of the Gods* (Arrow, 1998)

A well researched and enthralling investigation into the achievements of people who thrived in a remote period of pre-history.

Herrnstein, J. and Murray, C. *The Bell Curve* (Simon & Schuster, 1994)

A comprehensive account of the way in which intelligence is distributed against a range of population parameters. Hereditability emerges as an important factor. A useful background for assessing the roots of the True Professional.

Lee, R.B. and Daly, R. (editors) *The Cambridge Encyclopedia of Hunters and Gatherers* (University of Toronto, 1999)

Provides an up-to-date detailed and also valuable overview of aboriginal communities.

Morgan, Elaine *The Descent of Women* (Souvenir Press, 1985)

A well documented and interesting, if partisan, attempt to account for the part played by women in evolution. Favours the theory that the original habitat of humans was the coastal region.

Morris, Desmond *The Naked Ape* (Vintage, 1999)

The classic study of humans viewed by an academic zoologist with a gift for writing. This reprinted book that shocked many people when it first appeared has lost nothing in topicality.

Quammen, David *The Song of the Dodo* (Pimlico, 1996)

A comprehensive and racy account of the part played by mass extinctions in evolution. A notable contribution to understanding the evolutionary process.

Thompson, George   *Studies in the Prehistoric Aegean* (Lawrence & Wishart, 1949)

> The Aegean Islands and the surrounding coastline gave rise to some of the most advanced early civilizations. Their traces are recorded through legends or literary fragments.

Waite, Mary Ellen (editor)   *A History of Women Philosophers*. Vol. I: 600 B.C.– 500 A.D. (Kluwer Academic Publishers, 1987)

> The most authoritative record of the earliest writings of women, limited only by the fact that these writings survive only as fragments.

Watson, Lyall   *Jacobson's Organ* (Allen Lane, 1999)

> A valuable account of the relatively recent discovery of the part played by pheromones in human behaviour.

Wilson E.O.   *Consilience* (Little, Brown & Co., 1998)

> One of the world's most notable thinkers on the integration of the biosciences. Brings together inductions over different disciplines and develops the concept of co-evolution.

Index